W9-BLZ-737

Confronting Racism, Poverty, and Power
Classroom Strategies to Change the World

Catherine Compton-Lilly
With a Chapter by Todd K. Lilly

HEINEMANN
Portsmouth, NH

Heinemann

361 Hanover Street
Portsmouth, NH 03801-3912
www.heinemann.com

Offices and agents throughout the world

© 2004 by Catherine Compton-Lilly

All rights reserved. No part of this book may be reproduced in any form or by any electronic or mechanical means, including information storage and retrieval systems, without permission in writing from the publisher, except by a reviewer, who may quote brief passages in a review.

The author and publisher wish to thank those who have generously given permission to reprint borrowed material:

"An Award Winning Approach to Lead Safety" by Catherine Compton-Lilly is reprinted with permission from National Science Teachers Association, *Science and Children*, January 2002, Vol. 39 Number 4.

Library of Congress Cataloging-in-Publication Data
Compton-Lilly, Catherine.
    Confronting racism, poverty, and power : classroom strategies to
  change the world / Catherine Compton-Lilly with Todd K. Lilly ; foreword
  by Patrick Shannon.
      p.   cm.
    Includes bibliographical references and index.
    ISBN 0-325-00607-5
    1. Discrimination in education—United States.   2. Racism—United
    States.   3. Critical pedagogy—United States.   I. Lilly, Todd K.   II. Title.
  LC212.2.C66 2003
  370.11'5—dc22

                                                    2003021547

Editor: Lois Bridges
Production service: Kim Arney Mulcahy
Production coordinator: Sonja S. Chapman
Cover design: Jenny Jensen Greeleaf
Compositor: Kim Arney Mulcahy
Manufacturing: Steve Bernier

Printed in the United States of America on acid-free paper
21 20 19 18 17 VP 11 12 13 14 15

I dedicate this book to my brilliant coauthor/husband and our favorite young poet.

I am the dirt
The dirty dirt
I sleep all day and then say
"Don't put your fingers in me. That hurt."
I love to eat your footprints.
They taste wonderful.
I love tracking into your house.
It is a dazzling ride.
But I hide away
When I'm washed everyday.
So bye-bye dirt
And I'm gone.

C. C. L., age nine and a half

CONTENTS

Contents

Foreword

≈

Too many years ago to count without taking off your shoes, I taught in the same school district where Catherine Compton-Lilly now teaches. When I started, the city school district was in the last year of open enrollment. That policy was the result of a court directive to desegregate schools in order to alleviate the gap in school outcomes between black and white students in the city. Initially, white and black students were selected to transfer between schools in order to achieve some racial balance. Each morning busloads of black students traveling from the center of the city to the outskirts of town passed busloads of white students heading the opposite direction. This version of the policy lasted only three years, then it morphed into a policy allowing families to choose whether or not to continue the exchange. I arrived at School No. 1 during the latter phase, and as I recall, about ten black students rode the bus to attend that elementary school in a park bordering working and middle-class neighborhoods. None traveled the other way.

As imperfect as this busing policy might appear, it was based on the assumption that segregation and its consequences were public and not private matters. That is, because it was assumed that institutions and policies created the gap between students through separate and unequal schooling, housing, and employment, the federal government had the responsibility to act on behalf of those who were systematically disadvantaged. The purpose of desegregated schooling was to mix students by race in order to create some cultural understandings among them. If this assumption seems illogical, absurd, liberal, that's because since the 1980s the federal government has engaged in campaigns to erase the idea of the public from our collective national memory and to inscribe it with the idea of private responsibility for both wealth and poverty.

Perhaps you remember President Reagan blaming the federal Aid to Dependent Children program for the creation of dependent cultures? He charged that the academic (and income) gaps were caused by cultures that taught students not to assume responsibility for themselves or their learning. Later, President Clinton ended "welfare as we know it." Shortly thereafter, Richard Hernnstein and Charles Murray informed us that the gap was a mark of nature representing differing genetic endowments. Therefore, group-oriented solutions to social inequities were shortsighted at best and injurious at worst because they promoted people beyond their levels of intelligence. Accordingly, all hiring, school admissions, and government appointments should disregard issues of history or justice. William Bennett combined these two positions by suggesting that the culture of dependence and lack of intelligence created morally bankrupt individuals who threatened community safety. Currently, the federal Department of Education spouts the explanation that differences in brain functioning explain the learning gap. With each of these campaigns, the locus of responsibility for the gap in learning and earning is reduced from the society to the culture to an individual to the individual's cognitive functioning, and governmental action is eliminated as an appropriate response.

In *Confronting Racism, Poverty, and Power*, Catherine Compton-Lilly refutes these campaigns with the best data available—the lives of her students and their families—in order to debunk the myths on which these privatizing campaigns are based and to demonstrate that teachers as government agents can and should act to close the gap. She offers the words and actions of parents who recognize the public issues in the private problems each family encounters. Armed with these data, Compton-Lilly attempts to fight her way back toward public solutions to inequalities of outcome by demonstrating what schools could do to close the gap in learning through critical literacy. Along the way, she represents children and adults whose brains function well, who display keen moral characters, and who belong to cultures that support learning of all sorts.

Her actions have not and will not change the world, but they have changed the worlds of her students in ways she and they have just begun to imagine. If, however, you choose to take up her challenge to resist the privatization of responsibility for racial inequalities, then we have a greater chance for a better world.

Patrick Shannon
Penn State University

Acknowledgments

As always, there are many people to thank for the creation of a book. First and foremost, I would like to thank the children and the parents who over many years have taught me about teaching and so much more. We all know that the real lessons about teaching are learned the hard way through daily successes and failures. In particular, I must thank the ten families whose voices are featured in this book and who continue to work with me and help me to understand the toughest lessons of teaching.

Once again I need to thank my dissertation committee members who supported me throughout the research study that led to this book: David Hursh, Joanne Larson, Patricia Irvine, and Jane Hogan. I can honestly say that the experience of writing that dissertation changed my professional life.

I would also like to thank two amazing public school colleagues who read the manuscript of this book and provided me with invaluable encouragement and feedback. Peggy Campbell and Valerie Medley, thank you for adding your voices to these pages. Additional thanks go to the Critical Literacy Group at St. John Fisher College: Katie Sansone, Julianne Harris, Victoria Arena, and Allison Pietropaolo. These young graduate students, under the capable leadership of Sue Constable, also provided valuable insights and suggestions. Special thanks go to Robert Compton for reading and responding to yet another manuscript.

As always, the Rochester Teacher Center has provided me with opportunities to work with other teacher researchers and educators. Thank you for being an invaluable resource.

I must also thank Lois Bridges, who years ago suggested that I might have a book to write. Thank you for the invitation and the patience while I discovered that book.

Finally, books can never be written without the support of families. Thank you, Todd and Carly, for giving me space and support to do the things that I love to do. Teaching and writing are both compulsive activities. Thank you for accepting my compulsions.

SECTION 1

A Few Tough Questions

Take a moment to answer the following questions.

1. How would you describe the literacy levels of most poor and minority people?
   a. They often cannot read and thus cannot help their children with reading.
   b. They have no interest in reading and rarely pick up a book.
   c. They cannot read well enough to secure a good job.
   d. All of the above.
   e. They read for their own interests and help their children with reading.

2. In what ways do most poor families help their children learn to read?
   a. They practice letters and sounds with their children.
   b. They read to their children.
   c. They encourage their children to read.
   d. All of the above.
   e. None of the above.

3. Why are so many families receiving welfare benefits?
   a. The parents prefer not to work.
   b. Their families have always been on welfare and it's the only way of life they know.
   c. They fooled around in school and now they cannot get good jobs.
   d. The jobs they can obtain do not pay them enough to live on.

My research, with the families of my students, suggests that for most of the families I teach, the following answers are correct:

1. Question 1: e
2. Question 2: d
3. Question 3: d

I found that most poor families in the low socioeconomic, racially and ethnically diverse community in which I teach are capable readers who read a variety of texts for a variety of reasons. I discovered that these families are much more interested in their children as readers and writers than is often assumed. I also discovered that without exception the families of my students are very dissatisfied with the welfare system and would much prefer a job that paid them a living wage.

Take a moment to look back at the answers you chose. If you selected answers other than those listed above, you are not alone. Mainstream ways of thinking and our general cultural understandings about poor and minority families are deeply flawed and often based on assumptions and presumptions rather than in-depth knowledge about other people's lives.

This first section of this book will focus on assumptions. Chapter 1 explores assumptions that are commonly made about poor and diverse parents and literacy. Yet there are other assumptions that circulate widely in our society. In fact, assumptions are often made about reading. As you choose your answers to the following questions, take a moment to consider how noneducators might answer these questions.

1. What should young children do when they come to a difficult word while they are reading?
   a. try the first letter
   b. look at the picture
   c. look it up
   d. a and c only
   e. a and b only

2. What reading materials help children learn to read?
   a. the computer
   b. reading textbooks

c. comic books

d. all of the above

e. a and b only

3. What are the basic components of reading?

a. letters and their sounds

b. basic understandings about how print works

c. familiarity with the characteristics of stories

d. knowing phonic rules

e. all of the above

f. a, b, and c only

I suspect that most of the reading professionals I know would choose the following correct responses:

1. Question 1: e

2. Question 2: d

3. Question 3: f

While reading professionals share complex and sophisticated understandings about reading, we often find ourselves having to help others gain these insights. Most people in our society know how to read and thus believe they know *about* reading. However, the understandings that people bring to reading often reflect commonsense assumptions about reading rather than a careful examination of what actually occurs when children and adults read.

Assuming that the bulk of my readers are educators, I expect that most of my readers answered these questions correctly. However, I suspect that if I gave these questions to members of the general public, many of them would choose the following responses:

Question 1: d

I often encounter parents who worry when their children rely on the pictures to figure out words; some parents will even cover up the pictures to ensure that the child is actually "reading" the words. Other parents encourage even very young children to look up the words they do not know in the dictionary.

3

Question 2: e

Many people believe that reading textbooks are the best resource for helping children learn to read. My students' parents also tell me how important computers are to their children's reading development. However, these same parents often fail to recognize any value in reading comic books.

Question 3: e

Because people often confronted phonic rules when they learned to read, they often believe that these rules are critical to the process of learning to read. In actuality, most phonic rules are not particularly effective nor do they apply consistently to many words.

In this book, I will share the voices of parents of my students as well as my students to present many of the lessons I have learned about both their families and reading. I have witnessed how assumptions about people and assumptions about reading pervade our society. The close relationships that I have shared with these parents and children have helped me challenge many of my own assumptions. In particular, I have come to recognize the remarkable and inspiring people who are the parents of my students and how much they have to offer me in my quest to become a better teacher. Although I have changed the names of all participants, unless a parent requested otherwise, their words and messages are very real. Read on!

1

Assumptions About Families

When I enter the staff room at my school, I often hear teachers discussing the families of our students. Located in a high-poverty area of a medium-sized city, my school serves students from diverse backgrounds. Assumptions are often made, and blame is often placed on parents.

"These kids need structure; they don't have any at home."

"Cedrick's mother didn't show up for his parent conference. That's half the kid's problem right there."

"No wonder these kids can't read—look at this note from Keisha's mother. What do you expect when the mother can't spell?"

"The mothers around here are just kids themselves; it's kids raising kids."

"I don't think Jordan has ever seen a book."

When I hear these comments, I often remind my colleagues that we don't really know much about most of our students' families and our suburban lives are very different from theirs. I explain that we may not understand the complexities of their lives.

Yet even as I challenge these assumptions, in my colleagues' voices I can hear echoes of my own. Several years ago I left a position in a white, middle-class suburb to teach at a large urban elementary school that served a diverse student body. I entered a classroom that was familiar and yet very different. I couldn't help but compare my experiences with my new urban students to those with my more familiar suburban students. In contrast, many of my new students seemed more active, more frustrated, and less successful. The task of trying to help 29 students, several of whom displayed great energy and strong emotions but limited skills and an apparent lack of focus, was frustrating and initially overwhelming. The easy explanation was that the children's parents were to blame for the problems I was having in the classroom.

However, as the years went by, my motto became "You can't judge anyone until you've walked in their shoes." I did not realize that I, too, still harbored many assumptions about the families of my students. When I began a teacher research study that examined my students' and their parents' concepts about reading, I came face-to-face with my assumptions. I had to acknowledge that I too was subject to socially accepted ways of thinking and that commonly accepted assumptions about people living in poverty had permeated my own thoughts. Through professional readings, educational conferences, and sometimes very painful conversations with others, I have come to realize that my assumptions are not just the result of flaws in my individual psyche; they reveal commonly accepted yet seriously flawed ways of viewing the world.

Interestingly, it was the parents of my students and some very wonderful staff members who helped me understand the productive and positive role I could play in the classroom. The staff members who assisted me were neither teachers nor administrators; they were paraprofessionals, cafeteria assistants, and members of the custodial staff who lived in our school community. These individuals were willing to spend time with me helping me begin to understand the lives of my students and their families. Despite my struggles as a young teacher, both staff members and parents recognized that I cared deeply about my students; they supported my efforts to help children, offered advice and encouragement, and requested me as the teacher for their children.

In this section, I will explore assumptions that are often made about diverse families and reading. First, in Chapter 1, I will consider the ways my students and their family members are often portrayed in our society. Then I will explore the role power plays in the daily lives of my students and their family members and suggest a theoretical framework for understanding power. In Chapter 2, I will examine commonsense assumptions about reading and explore the roles these assumptions play in my students' lives.

Portrayals of My Students and Their Families

The media have contributed to associating a particular set of beliefs with poor African American and Hispanic people. Television images of people of color are often mug shots. Newspapers report on African American and Hispanic men and women who are allegedly associated with various crimes. Our weekday talk shows feature people of color, often from low-income communities, who are manipulated and cajoled by some talk show hosts to reveal the most sordid details of their lives. When successful African American and Hispanic people are glamorized by the media, they are generally sports heroes or music idols. Too often the sensationalized reports that feature these individuals focus on them as irresponsible, moody, unprofessional, drug addicted, or immoral.

Moreover, our society has a particularly ugly history of racism dating back to the mass capture and confinement of African people and the subjugation and conquest of our Native American populations. Faced with the unethical and inhuman nature of these acts, white colonists were left with the need to justify their actions by dehumanizing the people who were the subjects of their racist attacks. Thus, African American, Native American, and Hispanic peoples have been positioned and are commonly viewed as being inferior and less deserving (Gans 1995). Scientific explanations were created to prove the inferiority of the darker races, and intelligence tests were developed to confirm this socially constructed belief (Gould 1981).

Over the past two hundred years these themes have acted on our psyches; literature, theater, film, newspaper, advertising, and television have constructed almost indelible images of people of color as stupid, ignorant, foolish, criminal, and inferior (Nieto 1999). Despite the growing number of positive depictions of people of color in our media, those initial images remain with us and continue to infect our perceptions about non-white people. Similar depictions transcend race, claiming additional victims by virtue of people's physical stature, ableness, language, dialect, religion, sexual orientation, and gender.

While current depictions of deficit are less blatant, these perceptions continue to proliferate. Statements such as "His mother just doesn't care," "That family has always been trouble," and "I'd bet her mother doesn't know how to read" are thinly cloaked manifestations of these beliefs. These images allow us to blame the difficulties of African American and Hispanic children on families while society, schools, and teachers are absolved of blame for the miseducation of millions of children.

Attributing the difficulties of lower socioeconomic students to their families is not unique to American schools. Peter Freebody, Tim Forrest, and Stephanie Gunn (2001) describe the assumptions made by Australian educators about lower-class families. Freebody and his colleagues note four ways in which educators characterize the neglect that is assumed to accompany the experiences of children from low socioeconomic backgrounds. First, Australian educators often maintain that stresses associated with lower-class life contribute to the parents' inability to attend to their children's academic needs. Second, they also believe that there is an "intergenerational cycle" that links children's poor literacy performance with the attitudes of the parents about literacy. Third, lower-class parents are assumed to posses deficient parenting skills. Finally, educators cite material and cultural differences to account for the disadvantages lower-class children face. Freebody and his colleagues suggest that these assumptions about poor families need to be carefully examined by Australian educators.

Likewise, Eve Gregory and Ann Williams examine the myths "concerning the teaching and learning of reading in urban multicultural areas" (Gregory and Williams 2000, p. xvi) based on their research in Spitalfield, England. These myths include the equating of economic poverty with poor literacy skills and early reading success with a particular type of middle-class parenting. In addition, Gregory and Williams challenge the assumptions that reading difficulties can be attributed to a mismatch between home and school language and learning styles or that one particular teaching method is superior to others. Gregory and Williams explain that these myths about reading are not unique to the British educational system and are equally relevant to America educators.

Thus the assumptions that are made about the relationships among reading, poverty, and multiculturalism not only transcend North America but also extend beyond our national borders.

Defining the Good Parent

In my earlier book *Reading Families: The Literate Lives of Urban Children* (Compton-Lilly 2003), I included the following editorial, which was printed in my local paper. It was written by a teacher in my school district who was incensed that parents had been invited by our school district to annually evaluate their children's teachers. She writes the following:

> I have a problem being evaluated by parents who are not accepting their responsibilities. This year there was about 80 percent involvement at fall conferences, 25 percent involvement at open house. Fifteen percent of the class was absent 35–95 days; 10 percent were tardy upward of 37 times; 60 percent of the parents came in for spring conferences (mandatory); 20 percent of students didn't come the last day of school to get their report card or summer work packet. (As quoted in Compton-Lilly 2003, p. 2)

Based on generally accepted norms of parental involvement, this teacher has concluded that the parents of her students do not care about their children's schooling. She assumes that attending parent conferences, getting children to school on time, and attending open houses are evidence of good parenting. Furthermore, she assumes that failure to do these things is evidence of neglect. My own research suggests that these criteria may not be reliable indicators of parents' interest or commitment.

Living in poverty can affect parent attendance at parent conferences and open house events. Meeting with parents during traditional conference times—late afternoons—may be impossible for parents who are working minimum-wage jobs and cannot miss work to attend school conferences. Furthermore, parents who work nights and early mornings are not available to supervise children as they leave for school, which affects both student absenteeism and tardiness. Parents without cars and telephones are at a further disadvantage.

The information in this book focuses primarily on research I conducted with my first grade students and their families. In that project, I interviewed ten of my first grade students and their parents about reading. Over the course of the one-year research project, the families experienced many tragedies and challenges. When the project commenced, Ms. Holt has recently lost her eldest son in an automobile accident.

Ms. Green was struggling with the effects of the amputation of both her boyfriend's legs and eviction from an apartment with thirty housing code violations. Ms. Johnson lost her husband to cancer, gave birth to her youngest child, and became a grandmother via her sixteen-year-old daughter. Parents had also faced severe difficulties prior to the time of my study. Ms. Johnson ran away from an abusive father. Ms. Green has suffered from bipolar disorder since she was sixteen. Ms. Webster left the poverty of a small rural community to seek a job in the big city. Ms. Holt had been burned out of her home twice during her adult life and was starting over for the third time. These struggles left the parents of my students with challenges that I have never faced and that I cannot pretend to understand. Getting to know parents consistently reveals that each family has its own story and that simplistic explanations that focus on negligence and incompetence are generally inaccurate and incomplete.

Certainly, there are some urban parents who neglect their responsibilities as parents; however, negligent parents inhabit the suburbs as well. In the suburbs, many families have access to resources that help them disguise the evidence of their negligence. When parents can afford before-school daycare, their children arrive at school on time. When parents own a car and can take time off from work, they are more likely to attend parent conferences. These outward signs of caring are easier to fulfill when a family has a viable income and various resources. As a mother, I enjoy many benefits that the parents of my students do not. I can afford quality childcare so that while I am working I can trust that my child is being well cared for. I have a reliable car, ensuring that as I go through my day I will be able to keep the commitments I make without worrying that my car will break down or that the buses won't run on time. I can even resort to fast food or a restaurant on those evenings when the flurry of daily life prevents me from preparing dinner for my family.

An Example of Relative Power

The following story was told by the mother of one of my students. I had asked Ms. Holt if she thought that parents ever felt uncomfortable or unwelcome at their children's school.

> Sometimes. As a matter of fact, yesterday I had to go to school for one of my sons. And when I went there the principal made me feel

very uncomfortable because we were talking and then all of a sudden he says, "When your son was staying with his dad he was doing so much better. As a matter of fact, how long has he been back home?" I said, "What are you trying to insinuate—that I'm a bad mother?" I mean I got offensive right quick because my son was only at his father's house maybe six weeks and he's trying to tell me that since he's come back with me he's got that much of a change. I said, "No, that's not why." Then I went in detail [about] why he changed and then the principal made a total about face but he had just made an assumption and this was the first time I had ever met him. And my son *was* cutting up. He was doing wrong things for these past six weeks, which I told him. But he [the principal] made an assumption, I think because I was a woman and I didn't appreciate that. Cause then I thought to myself, I been in this here situation for 20 years. I really took offense to it and I meet with him again [on] Monday and I'm going to let him know I took offense to that. You don't just say something like that to me. [For] 17 years this boy has been going to school and the last six weeks he's been kind of cutting up. When did he leave his dad's? For 17 years he wasn't with his dad. And I didn't have any problem out of him. Now you gotta say since he's home with me now I'm doing something wrong? You know, I'm there trying to straighten this mess out with my son and then you're going to assume that I'm not a good mother?

In this example, Ms. Holt confronts the assumptions that have been made about her. While she clearly identifies gender as the basis for the principal's unfair assumptions, I would add that her position as a poor, African American, single mother also contributed to the assumptions he made. The principal, as a person of relative authority, utilized his position to present his interpretation of the situation without inviting Ms. Holt's perspective. In this scenario, the school principal is enacting power that is socially accorded to him based on his position within the school; Ms. Holt is left to defend herself. While Ms. Holt clearly challenges the principal's display of power, the assumptions and the relative power the principal has brought to the table position Ms. Holt in particular ways that make it acceptable for him to challenge her ability as a mother.

This is one example of the power that schools hold over the lives of our students and their families. However, the power that schools and school officials display is part of a larger social order that privileges people in particular positions while simultaneously privileging particular ways of viewing the world. Power-laden interactions accompany living in poor and diverse communities. These power dynamics exist when I meet with the parents of my first grade students. Whether I am aware of it or not, as a white, middle-aged, middle-class, female teacher, I bring power when I walk into my classroom of culturally and ethnically diverse students and there is always the potential for educators to abuse this power.

This book is about power that is often undetected by those who possess it—power that labels and positions each of us within a society that carries with it particular histories and particular ways of understanding the world. As teachers, we need to recognize this power and understand how it operates in our professional lives. In the following subsection, I will describe a few theories about power.

Theoretical Understandings About Power

Norman Fairclough (1989) believes that power is often both invisible and deceivingly innocuous. He explains that people are unaware of the most dangerous forms of power; these forms of power circulate unbridled through our social landscape via the ways people generally understand their world and the ways in which they act upon those understandings.

James Gee refers to "master myths" that incorporate generally accepted ways of being in the world that seem "natural, inevitable and unavoidable" (1990, p. 138). It is through these master myths that the existing social order is constructed, conveyed, and continued. Gee (1992) uses the term "discourses" to describe the way in which these master myths of cultures are shared and maintained. He describes discourses as incorporating particular "ways of talking, viewing, thinking, believing, interacting, acting, and sometimes writing and reading" (Gee 1992, p. 104).

Gee (1998) explains that it is through the mastery of particular discourses that people gain access to resources in our society. However, not all people's experiences are personally and collectively reflected in pervasive dominant discourses. This may be particularly true for students whose cultural, religious, and/or experiential backgrounds differ from those of people who ascribe to generally accepted, dominant understandings about the world. Children who are born into households in which their home discourses capture and represent mainstream ways of understanding the world have huge advantages in school and in the larger society. Other children whose home activities, preferences, mannerisms, and understandings of the world do not align with the world are at a disadvantage in classrooms and schools. In fact, the ways of being that some students bring to the classroom can be at odds with dominant, school-sanctioned discourses. "[Dominant] discourses often incorporate attitudes and values hostile to, and even in part define themselves in opposition to, these minority students and their home and community-based Discourses" (Barton and Hamilton 1998, p. 148). As Dell Hymes (1996) explains, the discourses that are connected to formal and academic contexts and institutions dominate over the narratives and experiences of people whose experiences and understandings do not align with generally accepted understandings of the world.

When Ms. Holt walked into the principal's office, she confronted mainstream ways of viewing the world, when she was defined by the surface features of her life that coincided with socially constructed categories of people. Ms. Holt is a tall, well-groomed woman of medium build who exhibits a flair for short and "funky" hairstyles that would rarely be seen in the professional world. Her clothing sports bright reds and yellows that would turn heads on a metropolitan street. Ms. Holt has a deep, rich voice and strong African American speech patterns that are sometimes loud and often accompanied by a contagious rolling laugh that punctuates the ironies she encounters as she talks about her world.

However, in the office of the principal, her unconventional hairstyle and bright colors are read as unprofessional, ostentatious, and slightly illicit. Her voice, like her clothing, is too loud. Her African American speech patterns are viewed as evidence of her assumed lack of education and presumed low intelligence. She is easily positioned as a lower-class, single mother who cannot control her son.

Features of Personal Power

As a white, female, currently middle-class woman, do I have power? Am I a person of privilege? Fifteen years ago, I would have answered that question with a definitive "no." I worked my way through high school, college, and graduate school, often struggling to repay student loans. I worked long hours in restaurants and bars to support myself and complete my education. *Privilege* was a word I reserved for my friends whose parents paid their tuition, purchased their books, covered their living expenses, and subsidized spring break vacations. Teaching in a culturally and ethnically diverse school, however, has made me very aware of the many privileges I have taken for granted. These privileges are unrelated to my personal efforts and accomplishments. My race, class, dress, physical stature, ableness, and language all contribute to positioning me as a person of relative power within many if not most contexts.

Perhaps a story is in order. Last summer I purchased a shirt for my husband at a major department store. However, when I brought the shirt home, my husband found that the shirt was too large. Meanwhile I had lost the receipt and then discovered that I had taken the shirt from the store with the security tag still attached. Now this was a dilemma. I had a brand-new shirt with a security tag that did not fit my husband and no receipt to prove that I had paid for it. Being the brazen woman I am, I decided that my only option was to return to the store, explain the situation, and hope for the best. My cherubic, blonde, six-year-old daughter accompanied me. The man at the register eyed me suspiciously and said, "We'll have to check with security about this." With trepidation, I followed the salesclerk to the entrance of a long hallway that led to the rear of the building. He told me to wait as he walked down the hallway and knocked on a door. A door opened and a large, intimidating man stepped out. The salesclerk spoke to him in a soft voice. Then the security guard glanced over at me and my daughter; he nodded and went back into his office. The salesclerk issued me a thirty dollar gift card to cover the price of the shirt.

This experience raises several questions. What did that the security guard learn through that quick glance that assured him I had not stolen the shirt? What would have happened if I were African American or Puerto Rican? Would I have received my refund if I were dressed differently, overweight, male, or accompanied by my teenage son? Just as the older brothers and sisters of my students are often victims of police profiling, I benefited from "profiling" played out in a mall department store.

Features of School Power

As teachers we must ask whether schools, classrooms, and teachers are immune to the practice of race, class, gender, and/or ableness profiling.

Regrettably, data suggests that we are not. Schools that serve poor and minority students are often underfunded, are segregated by race, and offer limited access to a range of educational experiences (Nieto 1999). Schools with a majority of students of color are 3.7 times more likely to be severely overcrowded than schools that serve mostly European American children. Nonwhite and Hispanic students drop out of high school at two to three times the rate of white students. The wealthiest ten percent of school districts in America spend ten times more per student than the poorest ten percent of schools. Furthermore, the proportions of teaching faculty without appropriate credentials is seven times higher in high-poverty schools than in wealthy schools (Johnson et al. 2001).

The school principal made assumptions about Ms. Holt and the mall security officer made assumptions about me. According to Fairclough, these assumptions reflect ingrained ways of thinking that position particular people in particular ways. "Such assumptions and expectations are implicit, backgrounded, taken for granted, not things that people are consciously aware of, rarely explicitly formulated or examined or questioned" (Fairclough 1989, p. 77). The power of these assumptions resides in their commonsense nature. As Fairclough explains, assumptions are most effective when their workings are least visible.

Lurking among these assumptions are generally accepted beliefs that things are "just different" in schools that serve poor and diverse students: "Our students can't . . . ," "Their parents' won't . . . ," and "These kids are. . . ." These phrases begin sentences that are typically completed with comments that align with generally accepted understandings of the world yet obfuscate the very real power relationships that define mainstream interpretations of the world. This "ideological common sense" (Fairclough 1989) serves to sustain established, inequitable relations of power.

Thus, the mainstream assumptions made about Ms. Holt are more than personal responses to her appearance, deportment, dress, and/or attitude. They are instances of culturally constructed ways of viewing people who appear like her. Thus, when Ms. Holt disrupts those assumptions and challenges the beliefs of the school principal, she is doing more than addressing a personal wrong. "What are experienced as individual problems can be interpreted socially as indicators of the de-structuring orders of discourse which occur in the course of social struggles" (Fairclough 1989, p. 172). Unfortunately, Ms. Holt's attempts alone are negligible against the dominance of mainstream ways of viewing the world, and it is questionable whether the school principal was significantly enlightened based on his interaction with Ms. Holt. At most he may have repositioned Ms. Holt as an "atypical parent," one who cares about her children.

Unfortunately, teachers, like most members of our society, are unaware of how systems of power operate in our schools and classrooms. We fail to recognize and challenge established ways of positioning people and labeling our world. Too often children in urban communities are viewed as deficient, difficult to teach, uncooperative, and troubled. Their parents are perceived as uninterested, complacent, subliterate, lazy, and negligent.

The intent of this book is to challenge our understandings of poor and diverse communities and to encourage teachers to systematically work toward unraveling our assumptions. In all societies, those people who control the society through money and might are the ones who are vested with the ability to label and explain the circumstances of others. Unfortunately, these systematic ways of understanding the world deny the existence of alternative interpretations and explanations for the experiences of students and their families.

2

Assumptions About Reading

People make assumptions not only about certain groups of people but also about certain cultural practices such as reading. Many commonsense assumptions made about reading range from reading being essential for getting a good job to good readers being "certain kinds of people" (i.e., professionals, teachers, lawyers). These assumptions about reading are part of our shared understanding about the world; they are generally accepted and rarely challenged. Like assumptions about poor and diverse parents, these assumptions about reading consciously and subconsciously affect the things we do and particularly the ways teachers teach and the ways schools are organized.

As Norman Fairclough (1989) explains, the power of these assumptions about reading lies in their commonsense nature. Unchallenged, existing practices are accepted as natural and normal. People who have not studied reading often accept assumptions about reading that echo their own experiences. Their ready acceptance of these claims prevents them from challenging either the validity of these claims or their results. These are the master myths that James Gee references that make these common assumptions about reading appear "natural, inevitable, and unavoidable" (1990, p. 138).

These commonsense assumptions about reading are often based on the premise that learning to read is a process of developing a set of reading skills. These reading skills include learning the letters and their sounds, sounding out words, and knowing words. While many reading experts would challenge the proposition that learning to read can be reduced to the accumulation of skills, it has a certain face validity. Understanding reading as the mastery of particular skills appeals to people not only because of its reductionist logic but also because people's own school experiences with reading were often focused on the mastery of these same skills, reinforcing the assumed centrality of these skills. Assumptions about reading are pervasive in our society, reaching across race, class, and gender lines; the words of my students and their parents often reflect these commonsense assumptions about reading. Likewise, these assumptions about reading are evident in national policies related to reading, including the National Reading Panel (NRP) report (2000a), which is currently playing a substantial role in defining and funding reading instruction in our schools.

In 2000, the NRP proposed to "undertake comprehensive, formal, evidence-based analyses of the experimental and quasi-experimental research literature" (NRP 2000a, p. 1-1). The culminating report identified five main areas of reading (alphabetics, fluency, comprehension, teacher education, and computer technology) and made recommendations relative to each of these areas. Significant discrepancies have been identified between the recommendations made in the full report and those that are reported in the summary document. As Elaine Garan writes, "The Summary Booklet misreports the true findings of the panel" (Garan 2002, p. 8). I argue that the greatest travesty of the summary report is that it continues to reinforce commonsense assumptions about reading rather than either findings of the full report or any sort of critical and in-depth analysis of the complex and socially situated practices that constitute reading.

The following are among the findings presented in the summary report.

- ". . . PA [phonemic awareness] training was the cause of improvement in students' phonemic awareness, reading and spelling following training" (NRP 2000b, p. 7).
- ". . . systematic phonics instruction produces significant benefits for students in kindergarten through 6th grade and for children having difficulty learning to read" (NRP 2000b, p. 9).
- " Fluency is one of several critical factors necessary for reading comprehension" (NRP 2000b, p. 11).

- ". . . vocabulary instruction does lead to gains in comprehension" (NRP 2000b, p. 14).
- ". . . explicit or formal instruction in the application of comprehension strategies has been shown to be highly effective in enhancing understanding" (NRP 2000b, p. 14).
- ". . . it is possible to use computer technology for reading instruction" (NRP 2000b, p. 17).

Many people involved with the teaching of reading have challenged the claims made by the NRP report (Allington 2002; Coles 2003; Garan 2002). Richard Allington, an outspoken critic of the report, explains that the "scientific evidence we do have about reading is now being selectively reviewed, distorted, and misrepresented by the very agents and agencies who should give us reliable reports of what the research says. . . . [I]deology is trumping evidence at the moment and teaching and learning to read will be the worse for it" (Allington 2002, p. 4). Allington explains that the NRP report is a "thinly disguised ideological push for a national reading methodology, for reading instruction that meets the phonics-first emphasis of the Republican Party platform and the direct-instruction entrepreneurs" (Allington 2002, p. 265).

While I completely agree with Allington's political positioning of the report, I suggest that there is an additional dimension that contributes to the frightening influence that this report threatens to have on reading instruction in America. As mentioned, this report identified five topics for "intensive study" (NRP 2000a, p. 1-2): alphabetics (phonemic awareness and phonics), fluency, comprehension (which includes vocabulary instruction), teacher education and reading instruction, and computer technology and reading instruction. These topics bring comforting logic and a reassuring familiarity to people who have learned to read in America during the past seventy-five years. The focus on alphabetics, letters and their sounds, echoes the experiences of many people who spent many hours in classrooms "sounding out words" and completing ditto sheets that directed the students to circle all of the pictures whose words begin with a particular letter. A focus on fluency alludes to our long history of oral recitation as a means to evaluate a student's reading as well as the memorable "round-robin" reading experiences in which each member of the class read a paragraph or sentence aloud while the other children waited their turns. Likewise, a focus on comprehension and vocabulary bring back memories of learning vocabulary words prior to reading a story and then answering the comprehension questions that invariably followed. While these topics of emphasis are validated by our own past experiences, the NRP's focus on computer technology promises that our children will be prepared for the future. Finally, the topic of teacher education and reading instruction feeds into readily accepted attitudes about teacher education as being less challenging and less demanding than other fields. It places blame on a community that carries a tradition of marginality and disrespect within the larger academic community.

The ways of understanding reading that are presented in the NRP report reflect the ways in which the field of reading is perceived by the general public. The ready acceptance of the NRP report among politicians and the general public is partly due to the fact that what the report advocates coincides with the public's shared experiences and beliefs around reading. Although these claims are being challenged by many in the reading community, they match assumptions that many people make about the reading process and learning to read. As Gerald Coles writes in reference to the claims of the NRP report, "the first lady [Laura Bush] accurately observed that it was traditional teaching, not any kind of new instruction, that this science claimed to validate. The fundamental message of this science was: let's get back to basics" (2003, p. 125).

Parents' Commonsense Assumptions About Reading

Like the authors of the NRP report, the parents I spoke with often expressed commonsense assumptions about reading. By far the most cited commonsense approach to helping children learn to read entailed "sounding out words."

> Ms. Webster: My big one [older daughter] does that to me. [She says] "I don't want to." [I tell her] "Sound it out." [She says] "I don't want to. I can't." [I say] "No, that's [can't is] not a word, you can. You can and you just don't."

> Ms. Mason: I ask him [Ryan] to spell it out to me. If I'm not sitting close by him I say spell that to me and he will spell it out. And I tell

him how to pronounce it. And look at the beginning of the letter and look at the end—just sound it out. If he still can't figure it out then I'll help him out.

Ms. Webster describes how she helps Tiffany sound out words and then remember the words she has decoded.

We sit down for at least fifteen to twenty minutes a day and I take a book out and I will point to the words and she'll say it and if she can't get it then I'll say "Okay, now sound it out. What does this letter sound like?" And then she will tell me and then we will go to the next letter and then we'll put them together and then we'll just keep putting them together until she'll say the word. . . . We'll go to the next page and then I will turn it back again [to the word they sounded out] and I'll say, "Tiffany, what's that word?" You know, because we will keep going back. I mean I may go to like a couple pages after that and then go back again and say, "What's that word again?" And that's the way she'll pick them up.

Other commonsense assumptions about reading involve the importance of repetition and practice. Ms. Hudson describes how she introduces a new and challenging book to Jermaine.

I read all the way through the book fast and then he read a page and then I read a page . . . so we did a lot of that there. Then I made him go all the way back and read it himself. . . . The next day, I brought the same book back out and let him read it by himself.

Several parents report using writing to help children remember new words. Mr. Sherwood tells Marvin's older sister to "Just write some of the words that you don't know." He explains that "We'd keep writing the words . . . she'd start to pick up on them." Ms. Johnson uses a similar strategy with David. "Well, I usually wait two or three minutes and if he still doesn't have the word, I'll tell him what it is and then I make him write it five times so he remembers." When I asked Ms. Webster if teaching Tiffany how to write words helped her learn to read, Ms. Webster explained her reasoning: "I think so because it's teaching her how to write the word and if she knows how to write the words, so then she's reading it." Each of these strategies presents reading as a process of using phonetic information to decode words as well as memorizing words. These approaches make sense given the phonetic structure of our language and the visual nature of reading; however, they fail to address how we comprehend, interpret, or connect personal meanings to texts.

Parents' "Funds of Knowledge" About Reading

Although the parents of my students do voice commonsense notions about reading, a careful reading of their words reveals that the understandings the parents of my students possess about reading far exceed these commonsense notions. Luis Moll and his colleagues use the phrase "funds of knowledge" to refer to "the historically accumulated and culturally developed bodies of knowledge and skills essential for household or individual well-functioning" (Moll et al. 1992, p. 133). While the families of my students possess numerous funds of knowledge in a range of areas, my research has focused on the substantial amounts of knowledge each family has accumulated about reading and learning to read. These funds of knowledge are supported by a rich array of resources about reading, including beliefs that pervade American culture, lessons that parents have learned from their own school experiences, and lessons that they have learned while supporting their children with learning to read. In this chapter, I will explore some of the instructional resources that constitute the vast funds of knowledge about reading possessed by the parents of my students. Additional instructional resources will be revealed in Section 2 as I expose twelve pervasive myths about poor and diverse parents.

Assumptions About Reading and Parents' Own School Experiences

Commonsense assumptions about reading often reflect the ways that parents and other people were taught to read in school. These practices often inform the interactions that parents have with their own children. Parents often describe using reading practices they learned in their own elementary classrooms with their children. However, many parents also learned very negative and possibly harmful lessons in school.

Ms. Rodriguez explains how her school learning experiences have informed her interactions with her children. She says that learning spelling words in school "was fun because the spelling words they gave us . . . was something I didn't know so I had to go home and study." She later created a spelling game that she believes has helped her own children learn how to read.

> . . . you say "this is a window" and you spell *window* and then you spell *door* and stuff like that. It's simple but as they grow up they be looking at it like, I learned how to read early. Yeah, and I learned how to spell early.

I asked the parents whether they thought using flashcards to teach reading was helpful. Mr. Sherwood remembers both his teachers and his mother using flashcards.

> My teachers used to do it like this. She'd flash it [the card] up like this [Mr. Sherwood holds up an imaginary card] and that word is *look*. And you didn't know *look*. . . . She'll put it back [in the pile], you know. She'll turn it over [later] like that and say, "Oh look at that!" and his mind flash back, right? "And what's that word right there?" "Oh, that's *look*.". . . That's real good. My mother used to do it like that [too].

Mr. Sherwood felt that flashcards were helpful to him in learning to read and explains that they are helping Marvin. Ms. Webster has similar memories of her first grade teacher. "[She] put the letters on cards and stuff and she used to stand in front of the class and make kids sound it out. . . . My teacher used to do that, Mrs. Olson. I can remember her too, Mrs. Olson." Parents are often comfortable with techniques that are familiar and reflect their own experiences with learning to read. These techniques reflect commonsense assumptions about reading.

While commonsense notions about reading were often apparent in the practices parents confronted in schools, there were also times when school reading practices taught parents alternative messages about reading. The funds of knowledge about reading possessed by parents include some insights and understandings that may work against parents participating in formal school practices. Educators must consider the possibility that parents' own school experiences may leave parents frustrated and disillusioned with reading. Consider these comments from parents about their own experiences with learning to read.

> *Ms. Holt:* Maybe it was that they *made* me read. [It was] not that enjoyable, they were trying to make me read.

> *Ms. Johnson:* . . . the class was large and the teacher couldn't [help us all], I guess mostly the kids was on their own. . . . I mostly taught myself really.

> *Mr. Sherwood:* They just give us the book . . . and you supposed to read it . . . and that was hard for me to get through. . . . I probably said "the," "sit," or "Dick and Jane," you know. I was just mumbling through the whole thing.

> *Ms. Hernandez:* It was hard . . . the words, how to pronounce them, how to say them but then it got better after a while.

> *Ms. Webster:* It took me a long time to read when I was little because I went to first grade twice. I didn't, I didn't want to learn.

These comments convey the frustration and sense of defeat parents often experienced as they learned to read in school. Ms. Holt describes how the teachers were trying to "make me learn" while Ms. Webster describes not wanting to learn. These parents position themselves as the recipients of an educational process that was forced upon them. Other parents describe large classes and having to figure out reading on their own; these descriptions conjure up visions of educational neglect. Parents remember school learning as difficult and frustrating. When parents find schools to be dehumanizing, painful, and destructive, they are rarely enthusiastic about returning to school to hear what teachers think of their own children. Efforts must be made to establish trust between the teachers and parents so that parents believe that their conversations with teachers will not be about what is wrong with their children or themselves as parents. Ms. Webster helps us understand why some parents might not attend parent/teacher conferences:

> I don't know. With me, I can't be there because of me working but there's a lot of parents that don't work; they [are] just lazy. They just don't want to go in. . . . They don't want to waste their time because they gonna hear the same old same old. That's what they feel.

While initially Ms. Webster places the blame for not attending conferences on parents being busy or lazy, she then describes how teachers contribute to the reluctance of parents to attend conferences. Are parent conferences merely an opportunity for teachers to tell parents the "same old thing?" How do we approach parents with information about their children? Are we careful to describe each child and his or her educational process in a way that is respectful, informative, and productive? How can we begin to form partnerships with parents where they are active participants rather than the recipients of bad news and criticism?

Contemporary School Practices and Recommendations from Teachers

Parents also reflect upon the ways their children are being taught to read. While some parents report that their children's teachers have taught them valuable ways to help their children, other parents find the relationship between home and school strained and difficult. Ms. Holt describes using a successful method for sounding and blending words that she learned from Bradford's pre–first grade teacher:

> It worked . . . it even helped me it helped me to teach, to help him. Rather than to try to go the way I learned. The "Bib system" [sounding and blending] was the way that they're doing it.

During my first years of teaching, I vowed never to send tedious and drill-oriented activities home with students, but in recent years I have sent home simple handmade flashcards of a few words and/or letters that individual students are learning, and I find that these materials are readily accepted and used by parents. Parents are often enthusiastic about using familiar materials with their children. When I asked Ms. Johnson about using flashcards, she referred to the cards that I made for David and described how she uses them:

> Oh, they [the flashcards] really help. He'll sound out the words. I'll hold them up and most of the time he can say the word right off the bat. Some of them he has a little problem with.

While some parents do use methods and materials that originate in school, many parents also believe that schools have changed since they were children. Some parents find these changes beneficial to their children, while others have mixed feelings and sometimes find these changes overwhelming.

Ms. Mason describes to her children how school was different for her.

> I notice it [is] different now and she [the teacher] can take more time to help you pronounce the words the right [way]. Cause I find myself with a lot of words I cannot pronounce right.

Ms. Mason suggests that teachers take more time with students now than they did when she was in school.

Ms. Webster also found her own school experiences to be frustrating; she feels that learning to read was a difficult process when she was a child and that the process of teaching children how to read has changed for the better. She explains:

> We went straight to the word. The teacher would go and say "Okay now we are going to sound it out." And then she would sound it out with us. That's how we learned to read. And it's just, I don't know, it was different. I mean look at kids now . . . and look at us. I mean we had to fight to learn how to read. And if you didn't know how to read then go back to school again. I mean, you know, the same grade over.

Ms. Holt agrees that the way children are taught to read has changed; however, she thinks that it was simpler when she was a child:

[It's] very difficult now . . . like we were taught Tom, Dick, and Jane and that was simple. You know it was real simple. But now they got the "bib" and the "bob" [a sounding and blending phonics program referred to earlier in the chapter] and instead of teaching them to read they [are] teaching them to rhyme. You know you got to read before you can know what this rhyme is all about.

In a later interview, however, Ms. Holt wonders if these newer programs might have made learning to read easier for her.

[They] couldn't try to make me read, I guess they don't have the programs now as they had back [then], we're talking thirty, forty years ago. Something like that. . . . She [the teacher] was doing the best she can. She'd get so frustrated. . . .

Finally, Ms. Holt feels that the changes in reading instruction make it difficult for her to help Bradford with his reading. She explains:

I give him [Bradford] to my daughter [Ms. Holt laughs]. And she have patience and say "dut, dut, dut, dut" cause she's just, you know, she knows how teachers do it now.

While some parents find teachers' efforts to support them in teaching their children to be helpful, other parents find current school practices to be problematic. Ms. Green expresses frustration with teachers and the suggestions they make to parents. "They got to give you some kind of instruction on what to do. . . . They say read to your kid so that's fucked up. I don't do that. That's too broad." Ms. Green expresses her frustration with the generality of teachers' suggestions. Reading to the children does not logically seem to be enough to make a difference in children's reading. While many of the parents in this study report that they read to their children, Ms. Green seeks advice that is specific and will reap observable results. Suggestions from teachers and current reading practices can support parents in working with their children, but these changes can also be problematic and confusing. These new approaches to reading can contribute to the apprehension some parents associate with school reading tasks.

As this chapter has demonstrated, parents use various funds of knowledge, including their own school experiences. The information in this chapter only begins to explore the numerous funds of knowledge about reading that parents possess. In Section 2, additional funds of knowledge will be explored; these include the parents' own reading interests, the reading that occurred in the parents' own homes as they were growing up, and the many resources that parents possess to help their children become literate.

Parents in this study may not always demonstrate their interest and involvement in their children's learning in ways that teachers expect and value. The funds of knowledge parents possess relative to reading may not be apparent within the traditionally defined parent/teacher relationship. Teachers must learn to listen to parents and to discover the many ways they support their children with reading. Teachers need to develop relationships with parents in which parents are comfortable, accepted, and respected.

The Format of This Book

The remainder of this book is divided into two sections. In the next section, I confront twelve myths that often surround poor and diverse parents. These myths are clearly challenged by the stories and insights I have gained from my research. The exploration of these myths also reveals additional funds of knowledge about reading possessed by the families of my students.

In the final section of this book, I will present some of the projects my students and my husband's students have been involved with over the past ten years. In each of these projects, we have attempted to connect the students' home and community experiences with literacy learning in the classroom. Projects completed with my urban primary classes include using students' jump rope rhymes to teach early reading, student explorations of reading in their homes, critical literacy projects addressing issues in the school community, documenting and writing about the jobs of my students' parents, and helping families learn about the dangers of lead poisoning. My husband teaches in a relatively affluent, primarily white suburb. His chapter emphasizes the needs for older, middle-class students to be involved in educational experiences that promote sensitivity to differences and compassion for others (See Chapter 10).

Section 2

Learning Lessons and Confronting Myths

I am a first grade teacher who has been teaching in a mid-sized urban district for twelve years. The projects referenced in this book are research projects and classroom activities that have taken place over the last ten years, during which time I taught at two different schools. My first school, Rosa Parks Elementary School, was a large, crowded school (850 students) located in one of the city's poorest neighborhoods. Ninety-seven percent of the children at this school qualified for free or reduced lunches. After eight years, I transferred to a school a block away. My present school, Henry Ford Elementary, is a "magnet" school that serves children from across the school district. The students at both schools are primarily African American, Puerto Rican, or multiracial children.

The insights described in this book are gleaned from a research project completed a few years ago. I interviewed ten of my students and their parents about the role of reading in their lives and their understandings about reading. All of the families interviewed were selected randomly from my class list. This became my doctoral dissertation and eventually a book (Compton-Lilly 2003).

During this study I interviewed both my students and their parents four times over the course of the year. I kept daily field notes, tape-recorded class discussions, and collected student portfolios. All audiotapes were transcribed in full with the exception of off-task conversation. The data were categorized based on evolving patterns of response.

I have slightly edited the words of parents and students for the sake of clarity by removing repetitions, false starts, and tangential comments. More specific information on my research study is included in the Appendix. The names of all people and places in the book have been changed unless the child's parent expressed a desire for me to use the child's actual name. At his mother's request, Roshawn Marble's actual name is used in Chapter 7.

A Teacher Learns

As I initiated my teacher research study, several of my own assumptions about teaching in an urban school crumbled. Although I had tried to remain open-minded about the parents of my students, I often found myself quite surprised by the results of my research. I had not realized how deeply my students' parents were concerned about their children's education. Because I had assumed that many were *not* interested, I feared they would not be willing to help me, a white, middle-class teacher, by agreeing to participate in a series of interviews. I could not have been more wrong.

I delayed contacting parents until the last possible minute; it was two weeks after the human subjects committee approved my project when I finally sat down at my kitchen table to recruit parents via the telephone. My trepidation was unbearable. What if none of the parents agreed to participate? What would become of this research project that was slated to become my doctoral dissertation?

I stared at the class list and thought about the relationships I shared with each child's parent. I was tempted to call those parents whom I suspected would be willing to participate. Instead, I resisted that temptation and started at the top of the list. I called Jasmine's number first; her mother answered the phone. In a tentative voice I tried to explain the project and asked if she would like to participate. "Sure, that sounds like fun. I'll do it." To my surprise it was the same with every other parent I called that night. No one turned me down. Seana's mother explained that she would be happy to participate but could not be interviewed during the next month—she was expecting a baby to be born the following week. I thanked her for her willingness to participate but did not include her as my circle of willing participants continued to grow. Within the next twenty minutes I had found nine out of ten of the participants and planned to personally approach the few parents who did not have phones to identify the tenth participant. The first parent I approached in person also agreed to participate.

When teachers come to know and respect the families of their students, it soon becomes apparent that explanations that blame parents are simplistic and that issues around parenting in poverty-stricken communities extend far beyond "don't care" and "can't read." How can teachers begin to understand that the daily struggles of our students and their families not only are factors in the inability of parents to meet middle-class standards for parental involvement but also are the result of systematic oppression? How can we value the resilience of families and build on these strengths in classrooms? How can we create educational experiences for children that meet their needs not only as children learning to read, write, and compute but also as people inhabiting a social landscape that begs extensive restructuring?

Twelve Myths About Poor and Diverse Parents

Myth #1 Parents Are Content to Rely on Welfare

Teachers at my school often assume that many of the families of their students are content to rely on welfare. Parents are sometimes assumed to be lazy, incompetent, unemployable, and uninterested in work. In contrast to these assumptions, while several of the parents I interviewed used welfare as a means to survive during difficult times in their lives, most parents voiced a strong dislike for the welfare system and strove to avoid having to rely on social services. While all of the families had been on welfare in the past, only five families received welfare at the time of this study. One family was receiving only supplemental benefits, and four families were totally free from welfare.

Parents found the experience of receiving welfare to be dehumanizing and the process required to attain benefits excessively intrusive. Ms. Holt describes being on public assistance.

> I think it's one of the most degrading things a person can go through. See first of all they [long pause], ahhh, they make you feel like you're not even a person. . . . First of all they have to know your mother's life history. You know, where was your mother at when she was nineteen? I don't know! You know, why ask me about my mother? I want you to help me and my children right [now], for this moment. I don't want this forever. I just need some assistance right now, for now, cause I'll

get me a job and go back to work. Cause I'd rather work, get my own [money] than wait for you [the government] to send any cause that every two weeks ain't going to get here and they don't send me enough to live on. They didn't even send you enough to exist on. You know what I'm saying? Like they say it's just temporary. And that's all it should be. And that's all they made it to [be] is temporary. [If] a person has to live like that for years and years they don't want anything out of life. They don't have any growth, they don't have any stature, and they have no self-esteem.

Although the parents in this study held a variety of views on many subjects, their response to the public assistance system was unanimously negative, with every parent echoing Ms. Holt, "I'd rather work."

Perhaps the ultimate story of frustration and degradation in relation to public assistance was told by Ms. Green. Ms. Green describes how the system can be used to regulate people's behavior and ultimately punish people who challenge or even voice a critique of the system.

They'll say to you, "If you do this again, I'll cut you off." They will threaten you just as well. And I'm serious, I've had this done. I remember I was pregnant with Shelia. I had, I was six months pregnant and I was looking very pregnant. They says, "We have to have proof that you're pregnant. We have to have this thing," you know. I looked at her and I said to her, "What do you mean proof? Can't you see by the way I look?" It didn't come through [Ms. Green's benefits were denied] and they were pissed off cause I said that [about being pregnant].

Ms. Johnson describes receiving public assistance benefits as being "very degrading."

When you go to different stores and things people look at you, especially when you have food stamps. Or even when you go to the medical doctors or whatever and you whip out the Medicare card and they give you a weird look. I've been through all that and I'm glad I work. Yeah, I mean don't get me wrong if I need it I'll go and get it.

Contrary to stereotypes about welfare mothers, the parents I have spoken with unanimously condemn the welfare system and are personally dissatisfied with receiving benefits. At the time of the study, several families who were receiving benefits were seeking alternatives to the welfare system through adult education.

Myth #2 Parents Are Caught in a Cycle of Poverty

The popular media often laments what is commonly referred to as "the cycle of poverty." We are constantly reminded of the responsibility of public schools to break this cycle by enabling the children of the poor to rise above their parents' stations in life and become contributing members of the literate, middle-class world. The assumption is that the families of my students are caught in a recapitulating cycle of undereducation and unemployment. My students and their families are assumed to have been born into poor families, to have always experienced poverty, and to be destined to remain poor unless the public schools remedy the situation for future generations.

I was very surprised to learn that this cycle of recurrent poverty was as much a myth as a reality for the ten families I interviewed. Among the ten families randomly selected from my class list a vast range of family histories exist. For some families the cycle of poverty rings true. Half of the parents I interviewed indicated to me that they had grown up in poor households. One parent moved to the city in which this research was conducted from a neighboring city as a young adult. Another attended school in Brooklyn. One mother's family moved from Puerto Rico shortly before she was born. One mother grew up "down South" and graduated from high school in the city where I now teach. One mother grew up in a small town in the far northern part of the state and describes her large family and poor upbringing.

However, the stories of the other five families challenge the universality of cyclical poverty. In fact, two of the parents in my sample report that their own mothers were teachers. Another grew up in a small northern town and then moved to a suburban area where her father was gainfully employed by a major local corporation. One mother lived in a middle-class area of our city and later attended suburban high schools. Another lived in a nearby suburb and attended both suburban and Catholic schools. Clearly, the families of my students have grown up within a range of social and economic positions.

Myth #3 Parents Are Often Children Themselves

Perhaps equally challenging to our assumptions about poor and diverse parents is the fact that the randomly selected parents in this study were not young parents. While we hear about the high incidences of teenage pregnancy in urban communities and lament the tragedy of "children raising children," the average age of the parents at the time of the study was thirty-five years. (This figure does not include Mr. Sherwood, who was helping to raise his stepgrandchildren.) All of the parents were at least eighteen years old when the child who was in my classroom was born, and only one of the parents was younger than seventeen when her first child was born. In fact, several of the parents have had many years of parenting experience and have raised older children who are now in high school and beyond. By characterizing urban parents as young and inexperienced, we deny the many life experiences that these men and women possess. Of the ten families in this study, six of the parents had raised children who were in high school or beyond at the time of this study. Raising children has undoubtedly contributed to the insights and understandings that experienced parents bring to parenting their younger children; however, teachers must also remember that raising children in urban communities may also be accompanied by frustrations and challenges as parents maneuver the maze of procedures and policies that accompany sending children to urban schools.

The school district in which I teach is a large organization with forms and procedures for every situation. The vast size of the institution can make simple processes such as changing bus assignments, obtaining a copy of a child's report card, or registering children for special programs complex and highly impersonal. As children move through school there are often conflicts, communication problems, insensitive teachers and administrators, differing goals and expectations, disappointments, and frustrations. These complexities affect the families' experiences with schools and affect the ways families experience the schooling of their children. Negative experiences that older siblings have had in schools can affect the experiences and expectations of parents and younger siblings. As teachers, we must be sensitive to how family histories of schooling can play out within the families of our students. Rather than a lack of experience, it is the kinds of experiences parents have had with schools that play a role in determining how parents interact with schools on behalf of their own children.

Myth #4 Poor Households Are Vacant of Print

Although I never asked the children to show me their books when I visited their homes, my role as a teacher inspired many of them to bring me books. Of the ten homes I visited, eight children or parents spontaneously showed me books during the interviews. When I visited Ms. Green, a forty-one-year-old woman, she showed me a stack of books that she had carried around with her since she was a child. A rickety shelf contained a half-dozen tattered paperback copies of books by Judy Blume and Beverly Cleary, awaiting the time when Christy would be ready to read them.

At Alisa's house, the living room was furnished with only a ragged sofa and a small wobbly table supporting a sixteen-inch television. The well-worn wooden floors were painted dark brown to hide years of wear. When I mentioned that I was interested in talking about reading, Ms. Rodriguez sent her son, Tyreek, into the back room. "Get that box of books from the back." It was over halfway through the first round of interviews and I was no longer surprised when children brought me books; but I was not prepared for the heavy box of books Tyreek dragged across the floor. It was filled with hundreds of books. There were "Little Golden Books," board books, Dr. Seuss books, textbooks, and discarded library books. Tyreek then brought out about twenty books from his bedroom and at his mother's request exchanged these books for books from the box. Tyreek's older brother asked to borrow all of the Dr. Seuss books, saying that he still liked them. Ms. Rodriguez refused his request, explaining that he was too old for Dr. Seuss. The older brother left and emerged from his bedroom with his high school social studies textbook, which he lent to Tyreek; Tyreek accepted the book readily. As we turned our attention to the interview questions, Ms. Rodriguez remarked, "There's another box just like this in the back."

In addition to books, many children have regular access to educational games, watch educational television programs, and participate in learning games and activities with their parents and/or siblings. Later in this book, I will describe a project in which my students became ethnographers of reading practices within their own homes. My students documented over twenty-five different types of texts that their parents read regularly. This list contains everything from medicine bottles to maps. The homes of my students are not vacant of print.

Myth #5 Parents Have No Interest in Their Own Learning

Throughout the research study, I was constantly struck by the number of parents who have pursued their education beyond high school. Although only one parent had attended college, all but one parent had pursued some education beyond high school and most had earned at least one certification (Table 3–1).

Table 3–1 Education Pursued by Parents After High School

Parent	Program	Certification
Ms. Johnson	Business program	Secretarial certificate
Ms. Hudson	GED	Not completed
Ms. Green	College/university Community college	Not completed Medical records degree
Ms. Horner	GED Business program	Started taking GED classes/finished independently Data entry certificate
Ms. Hernandez	GED	Not complete
Ms. Holt	Food service training program Home health care	Food service certificate Home health care certificate
Ms. Mason	Electronics training program Fashion merchandising Childcare program	Electronics certificate Not completed Childcare certificate
Mr. Sherwood	Printing program	Printing certificate
Ms. Rodriguez	GED Childcare program Computers/business	Earned GED Childcare certificate Critical learning certificate
Ms. Webster	Business program	Business certificate

Table 3–2 *Educational Experiences and the Current Jobs of Parents*

Parent	Program	Current Job
Ms. Johnson	Business program	Cafeteria manager
Ms. Horner	Business program	Phone company employee
Ms. Holt	Food service	Dining room manager
Ms. Mason	Childcare program	Preschool teacher
Mr. Sherwood	Printing program	Maintenance of copiers
Ms. Rodriguez	Childcare program	Preschool teacher
Ms. Webster	Business program	Receptionist

The vast majority of parents in this study are clearly interested in continuing their own educations. As Table 3–2 indicates, several parents hold jobs related to these training programs.

The understanding that many of my students' parents have pursued education beyond high school has inspired my current research project, in which I am investigating family literacy within households in which a parent has returned to school to pursue his or her GED.

Myth #6 Parents Do Not Care About School

Throughout this study, I have been awed by the parents of my students as they display an amazing degree of resilience in their daily lives. Many are single parents who work and attend school. However, many parents do not consistently participate in conventional forms of parent involvement. Like the parents in Sonia Nieto's study (1996), many parents of my students do not volunteer at school or attend meetings. They often delegate an older sibling to help students with their homework rather than working with the children themselves. My students do not take regular trips to local museums and only a few visit their local library, often in the company of siblings rather than a parent. Nieto (1996) explains that the reasons for failing to assume these traditional parental roles are multiple. She cites limited funds, a lack of previous experience in participating in these types of activities, and the parents' own negative experiences with school.

Nieto (1996) encourages educators who work with poor and diverse families to adopt a different definition of parental involvement. Despite their apparent failure to fulfill mainstream norms of parental involvement, parents teach children many important lessons about strength and resilience. They stress the important role school can play in attaining a better life. When they do not help children with homework, they monitor their children to ensure that it gets done. In addition, parents regularly intervene in school situations that are unhealthy or inappropriate.

Parents in my sample clearly demonstrated resilience and strength. They focused on their children's futures and the roles they played in helping their children develop the stamina and strength that children will need to succeed in the world:

> *Ms. Johnson:* I talk with him and I teach him. You know, not only in school but he needs to be taught at home. Even when you're out in the car showing him different things . . . you ask them [your children], "Well, what do you want to be when you grow up? What are your goals?" You know, there's a few different things. Of course he's at a stage where it's policemen, firemen.

> *Ms. Mason:* If he see[s] you trying that['s] gonna make him want to try it even more. But as a parent if I showed Javon that I don't care, Javon don't care so I have always showed him that I am really interested in whatever he's doing.

Several parents describe setting good examples for their children by going back to school to pursue their education in order to demonstrate to their children that possibilities exist. Ms. Webster explains:

> . . . that's why I'm pushing myself [by taking business classes] to make it because I mean then she'll [Tiffany will] look at me and say well mom did it, you know. After all them years, mom did it.

While parents may not be involved in schools in the ways the school personnel expect, parents do connect with their children's educations in other ways and feel that they are aware of what is happening at school with their child. As I write, it is February, and I recently asked the GED students I am currently working with whether they had met with their children's teachers. Only two of the ten parents had attended a formal conference with their children's teachers but each parent indicated that he or she had spoken to the teacher either in person or over the telephone and could tell me about the child's behavior and academic performance.

Myth #7 Parents Don't Know How to Help Their Children with Reading

Ms. Rodriguez: I make sure at least they read.

Ms. Mason: If they don't understand something [they are reading], I will try to explain it to them.

Ms. Webster: I try to help her sound it out.

Ms. Holt: We sit together and read whatever papers he brings home from school.

Ms. Webster: I keep going back to it and she's learning; sure is faster than I did.

Mr. Sherwood: We make sure he's got all his homework . . . and he understands what he got to do.

Ms. Johnson: We pass signs [when we're driving] and I ask him what it says. We're always reading something.

Ms. Hudson: I make him keep looking at the word and concentrate. [I] tell him to sound it out.

Ms. Hernandez: I help her try to pronounce it but she thinks she knows everything.

Ms. Johnson: [If he] can't get a word, I'll tell him what it is and I'll make him write it.

These comments demonstrate that the parents I have spoken with have many strategies for helping their children with reading. As described in Chapter 2, the parents of my students possess multiple "funds of knowledge" (Moll et al. 1992) about reading that are intimately related to their own experiences as readers and literacy learners. These funds of knowledge include instructional resources that originate from a variety of different sources. Commonsense assumptions about reading, parents' own school experiences, contemporary school practices and suggestions from teachers, parents' home literacy learning experiences, children's interests, and educational toys and technology all contribute to the funds of knowledge that parents access to support their children with reading.

On several occasions during my various research projects, I was struck by the sophistication of parents' understandings about literacy. As a part-time college professor, I sometimes found myself listening to a parent of one of my first grade students describe complexities and insights about reading that I regularly find myself explaining to undergraduate and even graduate students. Distinctions between saying the words and comprehending the meaning of texts, the importance of being able to hear sounds in words, the development of basic concepts about print, the importance of modeling literate behaviors, and the differences between reciting text versus reading words are among the insights parents in this study discussed.

For example, Mr. Sherwood makes a clear distinction between saying the words and comprehending what is read. He describes himself and Marvin's grandmother as being serious about reading:

> We mean business. Get in there and read the book and say it with me and stuff and don't play around. . . . You're going to learn it and you're going to understand it. And uh, you're going to know why the pig did this to the man or what[ever] . . . and it turn out that he understand good, you know. But see, he didn't really want to do it the first time. No, uh-uh.

Mr. Sherwood exhibits a thoughtful attitude about reading. He wants Marvin to understand what he reads. In a later interview he explains:

> . . . a lot of people read it but they don't understand what they read, you know. . . . They just read that whole paragraph and then when you ask them, uh, uh whether, um what they read about, [they] don't even know that.

Ms. Horner's words reflect an awareness of the importance of modeling the tracking of print. Ms. Horner explains how children benefit from being read to:

> I believe it helps them read. It gaved them a variety of words to listen to, to sounds and I read to my kids a lot. I have a book wide open so they can [see the words]. I can point out [the words] so they can see the words along with me.

Some parents also recognize the importance of modeling literate behaviors for their children. Ms. Webster reports that Tiffany "sees me reading a lot and I think she wants to read because she sees me reading." Mr. Sherwood agrees, "I'll look at the newspaper. I'll be reading it. Something will [interest me], I'll say, 'That's interesting, that's interesting,'. . . and I lay it down you know, and they get it and they read it and that's good."

Other parents made clear distinctions between their first grade children being able to read the words in a book and simply memorizing and reciting the repetitive text. Parents clearly favored "reading words" over memorization.

> *Ms. Rodriguez:* Alisa focus on, not sounds but memory. So she needs to get the sounds too. Not only just memorizing it.

> *Ms. Holt:* See, he memorizes that [the patterned book that the teacher sent home with Bradford from school]. Which is, I'm saying that's not wrong but he . . . sees the word *cat* somewhere else is he going to know that word [is] *cat?*

It is clear that parents do possess significant insights and understandings about reading. Parents use these understandings to create interesting and thoughtful opportunities for their children to learn.

Myth #8 Parents Don't Help Their Children with Reading

As many of the examples presented above suggest, the parents of my students do help their children with reading. Sometimes parents build on their children's interests by using books selected by the children. Ms. Mason describes reading with Javon:

With Javon it have to be something that is going to interest him. . . . If nothing [is] interesting to him, Javon don't want to take time to try to read or nothing. Javon is just that type of kid. You gotta find something that is going to draw his attention.

Similarly, Ms. Webster describes Tiffany bringing her books and wanting to read:

Ms. Webster: . . . she'll sit down with me during the day and hand me a book. "Come on, let's read, Mom." And it, I never did that [when I was a kid]. She likes to read. I mean it's one thing she likes to do.

Many parents believe that it is important that children are interested and engaged in reading. They often attempt to make reading fun and interesting. Like Ms. Rodriguez's spelling game described in Chapter 2, parents create games to make learning fun and capture the child's interest. Ms. Mason explains:

Like sometimes he used to have math problems that he didn't understand how to do it. Then I say, "Javon, let me show you how to do it." He get upset. He want to do it hisself. And I have to keep saying, "Ok, let's play," you know put it into a little game or something. Then sometimes he will get the hang of it and [sometimes] the games still don't work.

As Ms. Webster explains, "When they [kids] feel that it's fun to learn that's when they try to pick it up." Ms. Webster also stresses the need for teachers to make learning fun. "With teachers that are just stuck on the work and you know just pushing it and not trying to make it fun, that's when they [the kids] get bored."

As these examples and others presented throughout this book demonstrate, parents access rich funds of knowledge to help their children learn to read.

Myth #9 Parents Can't Read

All of the parents I interviewed for this study reported that they were satisfied with the way they read and that they could read well enough to complete all of the tasks in their daily lives.

While Ms. Johnson reports being an avid reader herself, she sometimes helps David's father with his reading. She explains:

> He never went to school. He only went as far as seventh grade. He is from way down south and he had to go to work. His father died at a very young age and he had to help his mother support the family . . . so needless to say, I do all the paperwork in the house, pay all the bills, read all the mail, but I help him too and he's doing pretty well. I mean he doesn't read the big words but he's doing pretty well. He can get by.

As part of my research study, I also interviewed two adults who were not focus parents in the study but resided in the households of students in my class. Both of these individuals reported that they had some difficulty with reading. One was the grandmother of one of my students and the other was the legal guardian of another student. "Getting by" is a theme shared by these individuals. Both of them spoke about not only the challenges they face but their resourcefulness in managing literacy tasks. Sharanta's guardian, a woman in her fifties, explains:

> In the grocery store you got to be sharp. . . . I know what we get and I go by the colors and the labels. . . . If I don't know how to read them [letters and bills] I call my daughter and I spell to her or she'll come over here or I'll take it to her . . . the bills, I get a money order for that amount. You know, I give [it to] the person at the post office, the lady knows [I have trouble reading]. . . . I get in her line and she'll give me the right amount.

Sharanta's guardian had recently gone on disability after many years of working as a school bus driver.

Although the parents I interviewed considered themselves capable readers, there are some people in my school community who struggle with reading. All of the nonreaders I have met through my research were older folks who left school early to contribute to their family's income, like David's father, or to care for sick relatives, like Sharanta's guardian. These struggling readers have been resourceful in finding ways to meet the literacy requirements they confront. Perhaps instead of criticizing those family members who have difficulty with reading, teachers should recognize the resilience and resourcefulness of these individuals.

Myth #10 Parents Don't Read

Parents reported that they enjoyed reading a variety of different texts.

Mr. Sherwood: Personally, [I like to read] the newspaper. The newspaper, um, science fiction, I like science fiction. I read those a lot. [I] Keep up with that. Mechanical books, I read mechanical books.

Ms. Hernandez: Maybe some magazines. I don't know, anything that interests me I guess. . . . My soap opera magazines.

Ms. Johnson: Um, I like love stories. I like the magazines that come through the mail, *Family Circle, Good Housekeeping,* um and [reading] US history is my favorite.

Ms. Webster: I like romance stories . . . it's the thrill. I don't know, it's like falling in love again.

Ms. Holt: The newspaper I read. I do that.

Ms. Hudson: I like to read the cable book, the bingo books, and then I like to read any, like read the paper.

Ms. Mason: Well, I read the paper sometimes and since I work in a daycare I love to do a lot of kids stories to the little kids in the daycare.

All of the parents in this study, with one exception, reported that they enjoy reading and that reading is a part of their daily lives. Unfortunately, as teachers, we are rarely aware of the reading lives of our students' parents. Too often we rely on our assumptions that define poor parents as illiterate or aliterate. As their children's teacher, I had no indication that the parents of my students were readers. Not until I went to their homes and asked them directly about reading did parents reveal to me their reading interests.

Despite my claims of rejecting assumptions about poor and diverse families and literacy, I still find myself wrestling with my own assumptions. This year, I am completing a study with GED students and their children around literacy. Again I found myself amazed at the notable reading interests of my students. While interviewing a twenty-three-year-old female GED student, I was shocked when she told me that she had just finished reading Dante's *Inferno*. Apparently her father regularly read poetry to her as a child and she had asked her boyfriend to buy her the book for her birthday. Analeah was able to speak very cogently about the book and showed me a poster-sized illustration that hung in her living room of the various levels of hell described by Dante. Once again, I had to reconsider my assumptions.

Myth #11 Parents Grew Up in Households Without Literacy

Contrary to the assumptions often made about families, the parents of my students generally grew up in homes that valued literacy and supported their children with literacy. Some of the ways that their parents supported them with reading are reflected in the methods they now use with their own children. Mr. Sherwood explains how his mother helped him learn new vocabulary words.

> I've got this method . . . that I use. She [Mr. Sherwood's mother] used it [too]. She always said, "If you don't know this word . . . all you need to get is the dictionary. . . . Tell me the words that you don't know.". . . And we'd keep writing the words . . . and we'd start to pick up on them. . . . It's good for kids . . . they got the dictionary in their hands . . . and they start looking up things.

By far, most of the parents in the study identify their mother as the person who taught them to read.

> *Ms. Johnson:* My mom sat down with me every night and read to me and she would sound out the words for me and that was pretty much how I learned.

> *Mr. Sherwood:* That's when I think I told my mom about it [having trouble with reading in school] . . . and she said, "It's time for you to get a library card and I'll help you out with that." And that's basically how I got through. . . . Every Saturday morning . . . we had to go to the library and we stayed at the library until we picked up on our reading.

Ms. Horner: I know my mother always bought me books and that was a definite. I've always been surrounded by books. I've always had a big bookshelf. She bought me encyclopedias so that when we had reports to do in school . . . all my information was just right there and we didn't have to go outside the home.

Sometimes literacy practices connect across generations. Ms. Horner describes how her own grandmother gave her helpful advice for teaching her son:

My grandmother told me [Ms. Horner laughs as she thinks of her grandmother], she told me when Peter was a little baby, she says you say the abc's to him and you count to him, one to twenty, every single day and maybe even a couple times a day so that as he gets older he will be up a little. . . . He'll be familiar with the letters and the numbers. . . . So that's what I did with him and at a young age, he was able to count; he can say his abc's so he was there. . . . [I] like that. Peter knew so much coming in already.

Parents learned a lot about reading and the process of helping children to learn to read from their own parents, especially their mothers. The grandparents and even great-grandparents of my students contribute to the literacy legacy of my students' families. Interestingly, most of the parents in this study reported that their mothers taught them to read.

Myth #12 Parents Lack Resources to Help Kids with Reading

While economic challenges are a part of daily life for all of the parents who participated in my research study, parents are often resourceful in finding ways to support their children with reading. Many parents report purchasing educational toys to help their children learn to read. Ms. Mason explains:

Like you know, I try to get him like those different things for him to learn by that way. And he has a telephone, now they got another— their own little personal computer. And I see that they are interested in that. Because they be trying to do the spelling pattern. You know, figure out what the missing letters [are]. And I just say you [should] buy educational toys, because they are the best.

Educational toys are a booming business in America (Shannon 2001). Phonics games, Hooked On Phonics, and products such as LeapFrog are targeted at parents who are concerned about their children's reading success. Washington and Craig (2001) note the tendency of African American parents to purchase educational toys. They explain that parents who in the past have been told by schools that they did not meet the school standards for literacy may rely on other resources, beyond their own judgment and skills, to support their children as literacy learners.

Some parents in this study recognized value in watching television. Ms. Holt describes a television program that her sons enjoy and that teaches them about science.

> But there's some interesting things on television though. You know, like sometimes on Saturday mornings . . . some science, weird science [shows] and you learn a lot of different things on it. All things on TV aren't bad. You know you can learn something.

Seana, a child in my class who was not a focus child, described a creative way her mother uses the television to support her in learning to read. Seana told me in class that kids "have to read what the movies are saying." At first I didn't understand what Seana was trying to tell me, but in talking with Seana's mother, I learned that Seana's mother always sets her television to display closed captions when Seana watches. She explained that this has helped Seana learn to read.

Ms. Green credits television for the progress made by her younger brother.

> I think television does a marvelous job. . . . You know my brother, he has Down's Syndrome. He learned an awful lot from TV, an awful lot. And he can read even though he's like, um, Down's Syndrome, like way down educable [mentally retarded] . . . and he can read *TV Guide*. He can. [He] knows every word in it and read[s] comic books. Stuff he wants to [read].

By far the most often mentioned technology the parents felt would help their children develop literacy skills was the computer. Parents felt very strongly about their children learning to use computers. Ms. Webster is completing a job training program that entails computer skills. She is adamant that her daughter also learn.

> I'm going to get a computer and I'm going to teach her, I'm going to teach her everything. I'm going to teach her what I have learned. You know, we'll do it little by little. But I'm going to get a computer. She wants a Barbie computer—$1,300 with all the accessories. She's gonna get it for her birthday. Her father's going to buy it for her birthday. That's what he told her. I guess I'm going to have to put half the money in cause that's what he told her. She told her father, "I want a Barbie computer." So if that's what she wants, that's what she's going to get because I want her to learn.

Ms. Horner explains that Michael's latest computer is "a little laptop with a mouse." She explains, "I know that whatever he does, computers will definitely be a part of it because he definitely likes to work with computers now. I just hope that he keeps that interest."

Some parents use the computers available at the public library. Mr. Sherwood describes how he taught himself to use the library's computers; he believes that a computer would be helpful to Marvin and his sister.

> I went to the library and learned myself, you know. I thought my house ought to have a computer. . . . It [would] keep him occupied. That's right, he be focused on something. . . . She [Marvin's sister], [it would be] good too [for her]. . . and when something a book, forget it [they are not interested].

Mr. Sherwood recognizes the attraction of the computer and the ability it has to keep Marvin's and his sister's interest.

Many parents felt very strongly that computers were essential for their children's eventual success. Ms. Johnson explains:

> That's all it is nowadays. I mean everything is on computer. Wherever you go there's computers—*everywhere!* Grocery stores have them, a lot of department stores, mostly all the businesses. Where I am [working

in a school cafeteria] I have to use a computer. He'd [David would] be lost without it.

Ms. Holt agrees. When I asked what types of computer skills Bradford should have, she replied, "All of them."

[Bradford should] know how to put them together, know how to take them apart and know how to do everything. . . . If I had my way, he'd know everything there was to know about a computer.

Clearly parents believe that technology can play a significant role in the literacy experiences of students. Commonsense assumptions about reading, parents' own school experiences, contemporary school practices and suggestions from teachers, parents' home literacy learning experiences, children's interests and enthusiasm, and educational toys and technology all intersect in the home literacy experiences of children.

Challenging the Myths About Poor and Diverse Parents

In contrast to deficit images of poor parents as readers, my research suggests that the parents of my students value reading. They have access to multiple "funds of knowledge" (Moll et al. 1992) about reading and they support their children as readers. While the funds of knowledge they possess may not consistently reflect current literacy practices or fulfill mainstream ideals of parent involvement, urban families bring many resources and experiences to the literacy learning of their children.

It is essential to remember that the parents of my students are carrying out these literacy activities within a mainstream culture laden with assumptions that often deny and denigrate their contributions. Furthermore, the assumptions placed on families often fail to acknowledge the stresses that poor families face. Society, schools, and teachers need to take a proactive stance toward the families they serve. In Section 3 of this book, I will describe some of my efforts to connect my students' home and school literacy experiences. Finally, Chapter 10 describes my husband's efforts to encourage his suburban high school English students to reach beyond their own school community and gain sensitivities to others who do not share their experiences.

SECTION 3

Building on What Children Bring

When teachers get to know the families of their students, assumptions vanish. Despite the complexities of urban life and the challenges many parents face, the parents of my students no longer appear to me to be deficit or deficient. Instead, new visions of families have emerged that elicit my awe and respect. The resilience of parents inspires me and the hope they display in their children is filled with possibilities.

> *Ms. Rodriguez:* She [Alisa] says she wants to be a doctor but I think that Alisa is more or less going to be a lawyer because she loves to argue.

> *Ms. Mason:* I think he [Javon] would like to be the head, the attention of the class. And I think one day that, you know, he do learn how to read good. And he complete school and I hope he continue going through college.

> *Ms. Johnson:* I have high hopes for all of my children. I always tell them, when I dies I want to die peacefully knowing that you have a good job, you're totally independent. . . . He [David] wants to be a fireman, the policeman, those kinds of things. . . .

While I listen to parents talk about their hopes for their children I am often struck by the many challenges that await the children and the many obstacles they may face. I am awed by the faith that the parents of my students place in their children, and I reflect on the possibilities that might exist if teachers could share this unshakable faith.

As teachers, we must strive to reach beyond the assumptions that society has taught us throughout our lives. We must strive to recognize the contributions of parents in ways that respect their experiences and their lives. As literacy teachers, we have an extra charge—we must confront and challenge the myths that exist about poor, diverse families relative to literacy.

Often, solutions designed to promote the school success of children take the form of advice to parents. For example, New Standards provides sixteen "tips" for parents. The first four are listed below.

Parent Tip 1   Read with your child almost every day.
Parent Tip 2   Regularly listen to your child read to you.
Parent Tip 3   Turn off the TV to read and help your child with homework.
Parent Tip 4   Make sure your child often sees you reading newspapers, magazines, and books.

(New Standards 2000, p. 30–31)

Like much of the advice distributed to poor and diverse families, these "tips" are remarkably obvious; it is bizarre to believe that parents really do not know to do these things. Perhaps most upsetting is that tips like these not only ignore the power differential that lies between teachers and parents but they exacerbate it. By sending these tips home to parents, the teacher assumes a relative position of power and knowledge. Just as the principal whom Ms. Holt encountered in Chapter 1 felt empowered to judge her, the teacher feels justified in assuming the role of telling another adult what he or she should be doing at home in terms of literacy. While it is true that all of us appreciate advice at times, it is also true that we can learn many valuable lessons from the parents of our students, and rarely are our roles reversed.

While there is no formula for creating equitable and respectful relationships with parents, there are ways to build on the diverse home literacy experiences that children bring to school as well as ways to engage students in literacy activities that are meaningful to children and their families. Clearly my research speaks to the tremendous importance of listening to family members and valuing the insights they share. Lisa Delpit encourages teachers to foster "true dialogue" with parents:

> This can only be done, however, by seeking out those [parents, students and community members] whose perspectives may differ most, by learning to give their words complete attention, by understanding one's own power, even if that power stems from being in the majority, by being unafraid to raise questions about discrimination and voicelessness with people of color, and to listen to, no, to *hear* what they say. I suggest that the results of such interactions may be the most powerful and empowering coalescence yet seen in the educational realm—for *all* teachers and for *all* the students they teach. (Delpit 1995, p. 47)

In working toward becoming a competent teacher, I have tried to listen to the families of my students and to reflect on their situations and perspectives. I have also attempted to design critical literacy projects that use the literacy experiences my students bring to school and to create a "third space" in which children, families, and schools can work together toward true collaborative learning.

Creating a "Third Space"

There are pedagogical practices that can contribute to the development of respectful and potentially productive relationships among teachers, students, and parents. One of my goals is to bring the home literacy lives and the school lives of my students together by creating a "third space" in which home and school interests can merge to create meaningful and personally relevant learning experiences. Kris Gutierrez and her colleagues characterize this third space as being a place where "alternative and competing discourses and positionings transform conflict and difference into rich zones of collaboration and learning" (Gutierrez, Baquedano-Lopez, and Tejeda 1999, p. 287).

In a more recent work, Gutierrez, Baquedano-Lopez, and Turner explain that an instructional third space is:

> . . . best characterized as respectful in that it utilizes the rich potential of the students. . . . Thus, the social practices in these classroom communities authenticate, integrate, and connect the classroom literacy

practices to the practices of the students' various communities. In this way, students' language and cultural knowledge become tools for learning. (Gutierrez, Baquedano-Lopez, and Turner 2001, p. 165).

Furthermore, in this work they identify three resources for literacy learning that teachers can use to construct a third space with students. Over the years, I have sporadically and unknowingly used each of these three resources.

The first resource involves using both the children's languages and classroom language(s). In Chapter 5, I will describe how I used children's jump rope rhymes as instructional texts to teach children to read. Using these rhymes involved talking with children about the need to edit these rhymes so they could be used in school; thus, we acknowledged and discussed the differences between the children's home languages and classroom language(s) in ways that required both the teacher and the children attend to the literacy practices that exist in both contexts while recognizing the existence and possibilities presented by different language practices.

Second, Gutierrez and her colleagues also recommend that teachers use student cultural knowledge as a resource. Cultural knowledge entered the classroom at many points during my research. My attempts to acknowledge students' cultural knowledge were not always smooth and were often unplanned. Initially, I was taken aback when children told me that "cops are bad" and that "you hit 'em back" when somebody hits you. When I first encountered these comments I was not perceptive enough to recognize that they conveyed particular types of cultural knowledge that are useful and perhaps necessary in the community where I teach. Perhaps the best example of bringing the cultural knowledge of the students into the classroom occurred when I asked children and their parents to document and explore the literacy practices that occur in their own homes. I was surprised by the variety of the responses. When students and parents witness a teacher recognizing and valuing their home literacy practices, it contributes to developing respectful student/teacher/parent relationships. I believe that over the years I have increasingly gained respect for the cultural knowledge that my students bring to the classroom; however, I continue to make mistakes, learn new lessons, and often find myself striving to make sense of the situations I encounter.

Finally, Gutierrez and her colleagues suggest that everyday classroom literacy practices can become resources for student learning. In my classroom, school reading and writing activities became personally and culturally relevant as students used reading and writing to address issues in their community. Writing about violence, the need for a new playground, drug abuse, and the dangers of lead paint all became opportunities for children to use classroom literacy practices to address personally and collectively meaningful issues. In a similar vein, Chapter 10 describes a project undertaken by my husband's suburban high school students that examines and addresses community issues that were meaningful to his students.

Ten years ago when I began these projects, I was unfamiliar with the conception of a "third space" as presented by Gutierrez, Baquedano-Lopez, and Turner (2001). While across the projects, we utilized all three literacy learning resources identified by Gutierrez and her colleagues, these literacy learning resources were accessed without a clear theoretical understanding. My attempts were admittedly haphazard and sporadic, with various projects relying to various degrees on one or another resource. The major influence on my work at that time was critical literacy.

Developing Critical Literacy Projects

Colin Lankshear and Peter McLaren (1993) identify critical literacy with the work of Paulo Freire, who advocated a "problem-posing" education:

> The students—no longer docile listeners—are now critical co-investigators in dialogue with the teacher. The teacher presents the material to the students for their consideration, and reconsiders his earlier considerations as the students express their own. (Freire 1986, p. 68)

In Freire's view, both the teachers and the students are learners as they coconstruct curriculum and the learning process by working together to read the word and the world. The following chapters will illustrate many lessons I learned through my involvement with these critical literacy projects. I learned not only about the various funds of knowledge my students and their parents brought to literacy but also about myself and the assumptions and beliefs I brought. The roles of teacher and learner became blurred as both teacher and students assumed both roles.

As Lankshear and McLaren summarize, the intent of critical literacy is a "rewriting" of the world in which people's "interests, identities, and legitimate aspirations are more fully present and are present more equally" (Lankshear and McLaren 1993, p. xviii). As Lankshear and McLaren explain, critical literacy is concerned with:

> . . . the extent to which, and the way in which, actual and possible social practices and conceptions of reading and writing enable human subjects to understand and engage in the politics of daily life in the quest of a more truly democratic social order. (Lankshear and McLaren 1993, p. xviii)

These may seem like lofty goals for elementary school children. Are six-year-old students ready to engage in discussions of politics and democracy? Perhaps not in adult terms, but they can certainly participate in discussions about fairness and what is right. They can challenge the expectation that they should live in poverty-stricken and violent communities while others inhabit large houses with manicured lawns. They can ask why their school playground is not safe enough to play on. They are entitled to know why lead paint exists on the walls of their houses and was used in the United States for fifty years after it was banned in Europe. And they are entitled to explore and value the funds of knowledge that exist within their own communities and homes.

In thinking about curriculum and teaching, it may appear that we have moved away from our earlier discussion about parents and the myths that have been inscribed on them. I do not think this is true. Critical literacy approaches by their nature have the potential to challenge existing ways of viewing the world. Henry Giroux explains:

> In short, curriculum itself represents a narrative or voice, one that is multilayered and often contradictory but also situated within relations of power that more often than not favor white middle-class, English-speaking students. What this suggests for a critical theory of literacy and pedagogy is that curriculum must be seen as a battle-

ground over whose forms of knowledge, history, visions, language, culture, and authority will prevail as a legitimate form of learning and analysis. In short, curriculum must be understood as a form of cultural politics that embodies the basic elements of a critical pedagogy that is both empowering and transformative. (Giroux 1992, p. 18)

An Overview of Section 3

In this portion of the book, I present several of my attempts to use critical literacy to create a third space in which teachers, students, and parents come together. My husband, Todd, also shares some of his work with his middle-class suburban high school students. Each chapter describes a critical literacy project with potential to connect families and communities to classrooms and schools.

In Chapter 4, I present the procedures and practices I use to organize critical literacy projects. Issues related to conducting critical literacy projects with young children will be examined.

Chapter 5 focuses on a critical literacy project designed to enable me to build on the literacy practices and language resources my students brought to school. In this chapter, I describe a project in which I collected rhymes and chants from children in my school community to be used as instructional texts in the classroom. This project provided my students with an opportunity to engage in reading instruction using familiar texts that were intimately connected to their home and community literacy and language practices.

In Chapter 6, I discuss how my students became coresearchers as we investigated and celebrated the many literacy practices that occur within students' households. By documenting their families' literacy practices, the children and the teacher become more aware of the role literacy plays in everyday life. When teachers express interest in these literacy events, these everyday occurrences are sanctioned by school personnel and are recognized as valuable and legitimate practices by teachers. This acceptance challenges the hierarchy that privileges school literacy over home and informal literacies.

Addressing real issues in the community is the focus Chapter 7. I describe a project in which my students examined violence in the community that surrounds our school. In this project, students not only learned about ways to prevent violence but also became activists for change.

Chapter 8 describes a project in which my students documented the contributions that their parents make to the community by exploring their parents' jobs. Although I created this project as an opportunity for my students to learn about their families, I learned volumes about my students' families and the community.

Chapter 9 describes a school-wide critical literacy project in which students explored the dangers of lead paint (grades K–5). Parents were invited to attend evening events in which the children shared what they had learned about lead and explained how to keep safe from its dangers.

Finally, Chapter 10 explores issues related to using critical literacy with suburban high school students. My husband's experiences as a high school teacher and examples of projects he has undertaken with his students are offered.

Critical literacy is not a singular practice that can be implemented according to a set of guidelines. Critical literacy entails a set of beliefs about social justice and ways of reading the world that entail valuing the knowledge that students bring while helping them use literacy to act for change in their communities. Each of these projects presents a unique set of possibilities. Some focus inward on the family and explore what the family brings to the classroom. Others look outward to identify and critically examine problems that exist in the community.

Each of these projects explores a particular way in which critical literacy can be used to bring teachers, students, parents, and school literacy expectations together. Each of these projects has had its own unique trajectory and concurrent learning experiences for me as the teacher. I offer them not as examples of what critical literacy should be but as activities that helped me grow and learn as a teacher. Each project has its own strengths and weaknesses and I, as the teacher, offer my successes as well as my foibles. With the exception of Chapter 4, I have presented the projects in the sequence in which they were taught. I suspect that my own learning curve is reflected in the projects.

While several of these projects were completed with young students, all of them could be easily adapted for older students. The depth and scope of these projects would only be increased. The final chapter of the book demonstrates the possibilities of using critical literacy with older students as well as the potential for critical literacy projects to contribute to the learning of middle-class students. The book closes with a brief passage in which I reflect on the information presented in this book.

4

Critical Literacy Projects

The children in my first grade class had just spent the previous week making a list of things they were concerned about in their community. I suggested that we would choose a topic from their list and seek ways to address that issue. The children were intrigued and their list was lengthy. They identified:

drinking
hanging with the gang
robbing and stealing
taking drugs
fighting
smoking
shooting guns
fires
traffic accidents
kids getting hurt
poison
stranger danger
violence
dangerous driving
cussing
diseases

Reading this list always sends chills up my spine. No child should have to worry about some of the things on this list. Unfortunately, many do. The community where my students live is not where teachers in my school choose to live. Overwhelmingly, we choose homes in the suburbs that surround the city, where we can insulate and isolate our families from many of the stressors that accompany living in a poor urban area. We have good reasons for wanting to shelter our own families from these challenges; it is a difficult life. This list speaks volumes about my students and their fears. I suspect that if my own daughter, a product of suburbia, were asked to create a similar list, she would include some of these same issues. However, living in the poor urban area that surrounds my school brings with it added dimensions.

Our first response as teachers is often to try to shelter our students from these issues. In our desire to surround our students with a supportive and nurturing learning context, we often downplay unpleasantries. While our intentions are good, we may be contributing to the problem.

My students literally walk past drug dealers on their way home from school. They report hearing gunshots at night, and several of them have lost a family member to violence. Memorials to the victims of violence are a common sight in the neighborhoods surrounding my school (see Figures 4–1 and 4–2). Drugs are a major industry in our

Figure 4–1 Victims of violence are often remembered with roadside memorials.

Figure 4–2 Elaborate murals are often dedicated to the victims of violence.

part of the city, with hundreds of people from the suburbs coming into the city regularly to purchase illegal drugs.

Paul Skilton-Sylvester, an urban third grade teacher, believes that the differences between urban and suburban experiences are grounded in racism.

> Our students face the stark reality of racism every day. Whether or not we find ways to talk about them, as our students ride from the dilapidated inner city to the immaculate suburbs, they *will* find some way to make sense of it. . . . [T]he point is that in our silence, students are left to understand the world using only their wits and the fun-house mirror which is popular culture. (Skilton-Sylvester 1999, p. 139)

Challenging Issues and Young Children

I am often asked if I believe that six- and seven-year-old children should be investigating the serious issues on the children's list. Other teachers ask me, "Shouldn't children be allowed to be children? Why rush into these adult issues?" Schools and teachers often assume that children should be sheltered. I don't agree. For many children, these issues are part of their world. By choosing not to deal with these issues in school, we create a boundary between the children's experiences at school and their experiences in their community. We deny the children's fears and trivialize their experiences. In their book dealing with community violence, James Garbarino and his colleagues write:

> Teachers must acquire skills that help a child recognize feelings, clarify issues, correct distortions, solve problems, and decide on alternative solutions. Such skills enable teachers to create an environment that promotes growth, self-respect, and self-regulation. (Garbarino et al. 1992, p. 182)

As they explain,

> Teachers can help children who live in dangerous environments cope with traumatic events and complex feelings and concerns. . . . The freedom of expression that is inherent in children's playful activity and in their art needs the adult's approval, permission, assurance and support. (Garbarino et al. 1992, p. 221)

Garbarino and his colleagues recommend that teachers, social workers, and community agencies work together to support children and help them work through the fears and challenges that they may face.

This is not to say that all of my students' lives are characterized by violence and crime. Yet because our school is located in an impoverished and violent section of our city, none of my students are insulated from these issues either. Most of the families living in the apartments and housing projects that surround the school are peaceful and hardworking people who struggle to do their best for their children; however, when faced with poverty and few job opportunities, some people turn to crime and drugs. The behavior of these few people compound the difficulties faced by poor urban residents by bringing crime into the neighborhoods in which my students live. I have found that the parents of my students often thank me for raising difficult issues with their children.

A Critical Literacy Project

From their long list, the children narrowed our selections to three choices: smoking, drinking, and hanging with the gang. The children voted again and decided to learn about gangs. Despite my stated belief that young children can handle difficult issues, I was a bit concerned when they selected this topic. Although I have taught in the community for several years, I know very little about gangs, and it was difficult to imagine meaningful activities that first grade students could pursue about gangs. I started where I usually do, with what the children knew and believed about people in gangs.

Peter: People go in their backyards and they see people [in gangs], if you don't say nothing they might kill you.

Jasmine: They go and um, if people have asthma and they smoke in front of them, they will get more sicker than that.

Sharanta: People in gangs are dangerous and they might even break in your house.

Lashanda: If you let somebody [from a gang] in your house, they might hurt you.

Jasmine: They smoke, they drink, they kill, and they take kids.

My students had some serious fears related to gangs (see Figure 4–3), yet some of their concerns were confusing to me. The children presented gangs as bad but attributed behaviors to gang members that seemed to me to be inaccurate or exaggerated. Taking kids and smoking in front of people with asthma were not behaviors I automatically associated with gang members. I needed some help in responding to their concerns. I was very aware that although the children identified gang members as being "bad people," some children in my class might have family members who were affiliated with gangs. Simplistic slogans that generalize about gang members would not be appropriate. For this project, I needed to seek out people who had knowledge and experiences that I did not.

I invited two people to visit the class and talk with the children. One was a former gang member who now worked with a local agency to support families in the community; the other was a paraprofessional in our building who worked with youth at a local community center. Both of these individuals visited our class and responded to the stu-

Figure 4–3 Kenneth drew a picture of gang violence.

dents' comments about gangs. These speakers answered the children's questions, discussed the reasons that people join gangs, and presented alternatives to joining gangs.

Like the project described above, most of our projects are chosen by the class through this process of brainstorming and voting. Some of the projects involve extensive work by the students as they read and write about a subject and then work to address that concern in their community. Other projects, like the gang project described above, involve information seeking but less actual agency on the part of students. Another project involved my students as ethnographers investigating literate practices in their own homes.

The actual design of the project depends on many factors. Some decisions are based on the topic chosen and the number of resources available to explore that topic. Other decisions reflect the depth that would be appropriate for first and second grade students and the time available during the school day to pursue the project. Some projects have gained a momentum of their own and have far exceeded my original vision. Others have been abandoned after a few weeks as the children lost interest or other demands competed for our attention.

These projects were inspired by readings I had done in critical literacy. The following components are evident in many of the projects we pursued.

- They address a student-selected issue.
- They are collectively relevant to students.
- They require students to use their developing literacy skills.
- They are designed to promote change in the students' community.

The projects generally consume fifteen to thirty minutes two or three times a week. Sometimes we work on these projects first thing in the morning to lend a sense of meaning and significance to the literacy activities we pursue during other parts of the day. Other times we have used the last half hour of the school day, when students appreciate working on topics that are personally relevant.

Lessons Learned About Critical Literacy Projects

Throughout these chapters, there are times when I was insensitive to my students and their families. There were times when I needed reminders to listen and when critical insights went undetected. I was sometimes less than reflective and occasionally authoritarian, but over the years I have learned many lessons. My growth in this area is due to the children and their families as they maintained faith in me and helped me move toward becoming the teacher I aspire to be.

5

Building on the Knowledge That Children Bring: Using Jump Rope Rhymes in the Classroom

The idea was conceived on a spring afternoon. My third grade class had just visited a local flower conservatory, and we were sitting at the bus stop waiting to catch the city bus back to school. To pass the time, some of the girls began to do clapping rhymes with each other. Soon every girl in the class and some of the boys were happily clapping out rhymes and verses. They did one rhyme after another, and I was fascinated by both their dexterity and their extensive repertoire. Some of the rhymes were familiar to me while others I had never heard before.

This was my first year teaching at Rosa Parks Elementary School. Before that I had taught in a nearby suburban school. I was looking forward to teaching first grade the following year, and I was already planning for the coming year. When I taught first grade in a suburban school, we started each year by having the children read and recite nursery rhymes. Because the nursery rhymes were familiar to the students, they provided an opportunity for the children to interact with texts that are familiar to them and with which they are instantly successful in reading. I had considered using these nursery rhymes with my current students but had heard other teachers at my new school lamenting that "the children in our school don't even know their nursery rhymes."

Watching my third grade students at the bus stop that day provided a welcome solution. Over the summer recess, I made arrangements with a community daycare center that was housed in a building adjacent to

67

my school; armed with a handheld tape recorder, I visited the daycare center to record the rhymes of the children who were enjoying the bright sunshine on the playground that afternoon. Four girls agreed to help. They began reciting songs as I recorded them. By the time I left, I had collected almost a dozen rhymes.

As I listened to the tape that evening, it was immediately clear that changes needed to be made before some of the rhymes could be used in the classroom; in some cases the rhymes included language that would not have been appropriate. I made minor revisions to the rhymes as I transcribed them and typed them out in large print so that the children could read them. I created books of rhymes for the children to read at school, with each rhyme printed on a separate sheet of paper so they could be copied and the children could illustrate the rhymes and take them home (see Figures 5–1 and 5–2).

The children responded enthusiastically to the rhymes. I explained the need to change some of the words so that we could use the rhymes in school. The children understood this request and agreed that we should do that. The children listened to my revisions and made suggestions of their own. Comments such as "My sister knows that rhyme" rang out as I presented the rhymes to the class. The students could often identify which words we had changed but seemed pleased to be using the material in school despite the minor editing.

Jump Rope Rhymes and Early Reading

I found that the large-print versions of the rhymes were wonderful texts for children to practice early reading skills such as establishing one-to-one correspondence between spoken words and text, left-to-right directionality, and the acquisition of beginning sight words. Some jump rope rhymes feature the "color words."

> Cinderella dressed in *yellow*
> Went downstairs to kiss a fellow.
> Made a mistake and kissed a snake.
> How many kisses did she get?
> One, two, three, four, five, six, seven, eight, nine, ten!

The children at the community center provided me with this version of Cinderella. With a little investigation, I located several other

Figure 5–1 Christina, a third grader, illustrates her love of jumping rope.

Figure 5–2 Zelda illustrates Teddy Bear, Teddy Bear, her favorite rhyme.

versions of this rhyme. In each version, Cinderella is dressed in a different color:

> Cinderella dressed in *red*
> Went downstairs to bake some bread. . . .
> Cinderella dressed in *blue*
> Went outside to tie her shoe. . . .
> Cinderella dressed in *green*
> Went upstairs to eat ice cream. . . .

Using these poems provided an important lesson in attending to the first letters of words. I would show the children one of these rhymes and support them in using the letter cues to determine which color Cinderella was dressed in and which of the Cinderella rhymes they were reading. Soon they could do this independently as they read the Cinderella rhymes on their own.

Another valuable lesson supported by the Cinderella poems involved the "number words" (e.g., *one, two, three*). Several other rhymes also featured these number words:

> I was born in a frying pan,
> Just to see how old I am.
> One, two, three, four, five, six, seven, eight, nine, ten!
> Bubble gum, bubble gum in a dish.
> How many pieces do you wish?
> One, two, three, four, five, six, seven, eight, nine, ten!

Some rhymes presented information that children were studying in school; some chants required the children to recite the alphabet:

> Ice cream soda, ginger-ale pop,
> Tell me the initials of your sweetheart.
> A, B, C, D,
> E, F, G, H,
> I, J, K, L,
> M, N, O, P,
> Q, R, S, T,
> U, V, W, X, Y, Z.

I used one rhyme to help students identify which letters of the alphabet are vowels:

Down by the bay
Say hanky-pank
Said a bullfrog jumped from bank to bank.
Said A, E, I O, U,
I know the vowels and so do you.
So ping-pong, ding-dong
Monkey-kong Junior.

Another rhyme could be easily adapted to practice either spelling or math facts. This rhyme also features an important dimension of African American language—the use of call and response (Moss, 2001):

ALL: School, school, golden rules
LEADER: Register [the child's name goes here].
Now it's time for spelling.
Spell *cat*.
CHILD: C-A-T.
LEADER: Spell *rat*.
CHILD: R-A-T.
LEADER: Now it's time for arithmetic.
Two plus two equals . . .
CHILD: Four.
LEADER: Four plus four equals . . .
CHILD: Eight.

Some of the rhymes were totally unfamiliar to me:

Policeman, policeman, do your duty;
Here comes the lady with the alligator booty.
She can wiggle, she can waggle,
She can do a split.
I bet you five dollars she can't do this.
Hop on one foot, one foot, one foot.
Hop on two feet, two feet, two feet.
Hop on three feet, three feet, three feet.
Hop on four feet, four feet, four feet.

Others were rhymes I had heard but in very different contexts. One rhyme, Rockin Robin, featured lyrics from a Michael Jackson song of my youth.

These rhymes and several others became a part of our morning routine. We used these poems as an opportunity to develop concepts about print, to practice early reading strategies, and to support the development of our classroom community. By printing these rhymes on chart paper I could draw the children's attention to specific concepts about print or particular words to be studied. The books of rhymes were made available to the children in our book corner. By moving a table to the side of the room, we created a "jump rope center" where the children could jump rope during center time while chanting these rhymes.

Rhymes from My Students and Their Parents

For homework one weekend, the children asked their parents, grandparents, aunts, and uncles if they knew any rhymes we could add to our collection. Children brought in old favorites including "Miss Mary Mack," a traditional African American chant, and "When I Was Five" by A. A. Milne (1992).

However, surprises still awaited me. The following year, I planned to repeat the process with my new group of first grade students. I decided that I would have the children use the rhymes that had been collected during the previous year and then supplement these rhymes with ones that they knew.

When I asked the children if they knew any other rhymes, the answer was a resounding "Yes!" Both the boys and girls were excited (see Figure 5–3). I was surprised by the variety of cultural resources they accessed. I quickly realized that by limiting our study of rhymes to jump rope and clapping rhymes during the prior year, I had neglected many of the linguistic, rhythmic, and musical resources my children possessed. During this second year the children shared with me some of the same rhymes I had collected during the first year but also enthusiastically offered "The Barney Song" from television, a version of the theme from "Popeye the Sailor Man," "Twinkle, Twinkle, Little Star," "Ring Around the Rosy," and "Humpty Dumpty." The new jump rope rhymes included one that has its roots in the influential African American churches:

One, two, three,
The devil's after me.
Four, five, six,

Figure 5–3 Terrell's picture shows that boys can jump rope too!

He's always shooting sticks.
Seven, eight, nine,
He misses every time.
Hallelujah, hallelujah, amen.

By including traditional nursery rhymes such as "Twinkle, Twinkle, Little Star," "Ring Around the Rosy," and "Humpty Dumpty," the children in my classroom very clearly challenged the voices of the teachers I encountered my first year at Rosa Parks School when they claimed that my students would not know nursery rhymes. Many of my students did know some traditional nursery rhymes—and they knew much, much more. Over the years, these rhymes have become a staple in my classroom, and each year the children continue to contribute to our growing collection of rhymes, chants, and songs.

A Lesson Learned About Language

There is an important lesson to be learned through this project. While teachers in my school continue to complain that our students are "language deprived" or "language deficient," I continue to be impressed by the rich linguistic resources my students bring to the classroom. They may not always bring the traditional nursery rhymes that the teachers at my school expect and value, but they do bring unique and engaging language that fulfills all the functions of traditional nursery rhymes.

In recent years, Reid Lyon (1997) has identified poor children as being deficient in phonemic awareness. I find this conclusion difficult to accept as I witness the extensive linguistic resources of my students. I cannot help but wonder if the ability of my students to recite, rewrite, and create rhymes, chants, and songs is not adequately reflected in the phonemic awareness assessments that we offer.

6

Student Ethnographers Studying Reading

First grade has an aura all its own; it is the year when many children learn to read. First graders understand this, and they arrive at school excited and enthused about reading. During the first week of school, I ask my students a very important question, "Why is it important that you learn to read?" Their responses reveal the importance of reading to the children and perhaps a bit of naivete about what reading is and how you learn it:

Christy: To learn the words and letters.

Lashanda: Our mothers and fathers might want to hear us read.

David: Because it's learning.

Peter: You need to go to the highest grade you can go to and you need to learn to read your mail.

Seana: So you can read and stuff and you can learn how to do your homework and read it by yourself.

Ashley: So you can go to first grade and you can get bigger and bigger and go to second grade and high school.

Although the children's reasons for learning to read clearly reflect their six-year-old perspectives in terms of promotion to higher grades, independence with reading, and the relationships they share with their parents, they clearly value reading and view it as an essential skill. Based on this understanding between myself and my students, we began to investigate reading in our school, community, and homes.

Learning About Reading in My Students' Families

Each year we take a literacy walk through the school and then through the neighborhood surrounding our school (Taylor 2000). We take photographs of signs in the school's hallways and in the neighborhood. As a class, we add words to the pictures describing the importance of each sign. These photographs are collected in class-made books. Although in September many of my first grade readers are in the beginning stages of learning to read, the contexts that surround the signs provide many clues, and the children quickly discover that the photographs enable them to read the books we make. These books capture the students' thoughts about the signs they encounter. Under a photograph of the sign for the girls' bathroom, the caption reads, "This sign is important so you know which bathroom to use."

After reflecting on the role of print in the school and the community, the children are asked to investigate and report on all the different things their parents read at home. We have been keeping a list and it has grown over the years:

medicine bottles

notes

labels

bedtime stories

recipes

poems

street signs

words on TV

maps

numbers

cookbooks

library books

books

coloring books

newspapers

school papers

dictionaries

signs at school

bibles

T-shirts

books about cars

magazines

signs in stores

charts

posters

books at church

papers from daycare

Parents and Reading

Once the children begin to recognize the vast amounts of reading their parents do, they craft questions for their parents to answer about reading. The students' questions are compiled in surveys that are sent home for their parents to complete. One class brainstormed the following questions for their parents:

How did you learn to read?

Who taught you to read?

What helped you the most when you first learned to read?

What do you think teachers should be doing to help children learn to read?

When the survey was sent home, several parents responded. Based on the answers to the first question of the survey, another book was written, entitled "How Our Parents Learned to Read." Each page contained one parent's response; the children illustrated the pages. The text reads as follows:

> Some parents learned to read from their parents.
>
> Some parents learned to read from their teachers.
>
> Some parents learned to read from their preschool teachers.
>
> Some parents learned to read from their great-grandmothers.
>
> Some parents learned to read from their grandmothers.
>
> Some parents learned to read from their mothers.

By far most of the parents of my students identified their mother as the person who taught them to read. I was surprised by this finding. Not only did the surveys help the children learn about the literate lives of their parents but I also gained new insights. While I had always assumed that I was the person responsible for teaching most of my students to read, I now recognize that there are many people supporting my students including fathers (see Figure 6–1). In fact, the parents in

Figure 6–1 Ian captures his father reading him a story.

my own research study also most often credit their mothers, rather than their teachers, as the person who taught them to read.

Children and Reading

Some years, the children also brainstorm questions for the class to answer. A group of students recently came up with the following questions, which they then attempted to answer.

> How do you learn to read?
> What things can we read?
> What words can we read?
> What should we do when we get stuck on a word?

We spent a few minutes each morning recording possible answers to these questions on chart paper. The first question revealed a range of interesting responses. Some of the responses reflected various decoding strategies:

> To learn to read, kids should find little words in big words.
> To learn to read, kids should sound out words.
> To learn to read, kids should know the ABC's.
> To learn to read, kids should look at the words.
> To learn to read, kids should look at the pictures.

Others advocated particular activities:

> To learn to read, kids should listen to books on tape.
> To learn to read, kids should practice reading.

Still others identified classroom behavior or the students' attitudes as being critical:

> To learn to read, kids should sit still.
> To learn to read, kids should keep trying.
> To learn to read, kids should not play.
> To learn to read, kids should pay attention.

The advice that the children gave to each other about learning to read is fascinating to me as their teacher. Some of their advice promoted reading strategies that I do not use. For example, I do not ask the children in my room to "sound out" words. I find that request to be rather general and too often becomes children's only reading strategy. Instead, I ask children to use the first letter, check the ending of a word, or find a part of the word that they know. In addition, the association they make between learning to read and sitting still caused me to reexamine how I respond to children when I am teaching reading. Their comments made me aware of the things I say when I am teaching. Reminders such as "Sit up so you can learn" and "Pay attention so you know what to do" take on a new dimension when children assume that these behaviors are directly linked to learning to read.

Perhaps the most helpful answers were shared when at the end of the unit I asked the children, "What should teachers do to teach children to read?" The class wrote the following:

> To teach kids to read, teachers should teach finding little words in big words.
>
> To teach kids to read, teachers should have kids help each other.
>
> To teach kids to read, teachers should use songs.
>
> To teach kids to read, teachers should read books to kids.
>
> To teach kids to read, teachers should teach the letters and the sounds.
>
> Better advice would be difficult to find in a reading textbook.

Lessons Learned About Reading

There are three significant issues raised by this unit of study. First, as teachers learn about the reading that occurs in their students' homes and communities, the teacher can begin to construct a more thoughtful view of his or her students and their families as readers. As the list of things that parents read grows and children and parents continue to offer thoughtful insights about reading, children and families are redefined as readers. Second, by asking the parents to share their reading experiences, teachers display respect for parents and the literacies they possess. Small acts like this can begin to redefine the teacher/parent relationship. Finally, by investigating the reading activities that occur in their own homes, students will begin to value activities that they may have viewed in the past as ordinary and unremarkable. When the teacher shows respect for the reading activities of children's parents, the children can begin to view these activities as valued by school personnel. Rather than viewing their parents as deficient in terms of school norms, both teachers and children recognize their parents as literate and purposeful readers.

Hopefully, through activities such as this, teachers can begin to carve out a "third space" in which school and family literacies can coexist and complement each other helping children to view themselves as readers (see Figure 6–2). Expecting children and parents to accept, value, and adopt school literacies will happen only when schools and teachers can do the same. We must learn to acknowledge and value the home literacies of families. Learning about families as readers has the potential to begin that process.

Figure 6–2 Kayla expresses her love for reading.

7

Addressing Real Issues in Communities: Fighting Violence

Yo why you place me in a world thats so cold, I pray to you as I walk down this devil road / It's like you had a tight hold but you let go as we got further down the road / It feels like I sold my soul and all I seen was my shady past / I'm asking you for guidance back to the light but none given / On my journey down the dark street I see how I'm living / bust guns on making money off of drug dealing / I feel like you abandoned me / and kept me away from you / put me in harms way knowing what the devil a do / but I'm back asking questions like what should I do / I get a blank response / No answer coming back from you / I'm stuck in a position and I don't know what to do / Forget it I'm gonna do what I know how, bust my gun / even if it means leave my enemies on the run / I trusted you as the heavenly father but you let me down / It's okay!!! I'm in good hands now / I roll with thugs that's the life you chose for me.

—Roshawn Marble, 4 / 9 / 01

These words were written by one of my former students when he was 17 years old. A year and a half later Roshawn Marble was dead. The paper read: "Marble was found by police lying on the driveway of a house with a gunshot wound to the chest" (Blackwell, 2003).

I remember Roshawn as an extremely bright and often frustratingly active second grader. He was interested in everything but often did not follow through on what he started; he was constantly moving on to something else. When I visited the funeral home, copies of

Roshawn's rap had been carefully photocopied and placed on a table beside Roshawn's coffin along with a poem that his stepfather had written in Roshawn's memory. Roshawn's power with words reflects one of the many gifts that Roshawn brought to this world and reminds us of the incredible loss his death brings. It was a few years after Roshawn was in my class that my students chose to do a project to address violence in our school community.

Children Investigating Violence

Violence is a major problem in urban communities. Last year in our city 41 people were killed through violent acts. Almost a quarter of these deaths occurred in the neighborhood where I teach. Although many of my students have never encountered violence directly, it is a terrible legacy of the community in which they live and go to school (see Figure 7–1).

Figure 7–1 Jahronda depicts a violent confrontation in her drawing.

When the project began, my students had no idea that violence would occur very close to home. It was mid-fall, just as my students were beginning their project on violence, when a middle school student in our district was stabbed to death by a fellow student as she got off her school bus. Evidently, a dispute over a boy was at the core of the disagreement. Needless to say, the city school district and the city reeled with shock and grief. We wrote a simple letter to Rachel's mother and sent flowers:

Dear Ms. Johnson,
We are sorry that Rachel died. Do you visit her grave? We saw her picture in the paper. We hope you like the flowers.

Ms. Lilly's Class
Grade 1
Rosa Parks School

It was more than a month later when we received a reply thanking us for the flowers. Ms. Johnson very honestly described her difficulty with visiting Rachel's grave. She emphasized the need for my students to learn from this experience and to seek better ways to solve problems. The children listened closely as I read the letter. A very honest and moving discussion about violence followed.

As we spoke, it became obvious that my students had many questions about violence. I scribed our questions onto chart paper. "Why do people do violence?" "Why do people have guns?" "What happens when a bullet hits your heart?" and "What happens when you get buried?" Together we crafted an answer to each question.

The children also made books that incorporated patterned text. For example, they made a book entitled "What Is Violence?" that used the pattern "_____ is violence" on each page. Another patterned book was entitled "Solving Problems." Students completed the sentence "We can solve problems by _____" with phrases that included "telling people how you feel," "moving away," and "talking to people (see Figure 7–2)." Using a pattern as the basis for writing with young children enables all children to participate in the writing despite differences in writing experience and ability. In addition, it has the fringe benefit of creating a class text that even the most novice readers can manage. The students were invited to illustrate each page, and the books became compelling additions to the classroom library.

We can solve problems by telling people how you feel.

Figure 7–2 Marvin recommends an alternative to violence.

Learning from Community Members

Many community resources were used throughout this project. In our city a number of organizations are working for peace in our community. Representatives from several of these organizations came to speak with the children. One of our guest speakers is a local organizer who became involved with violence prevention when her own son became a victim of violence. She spoke with the students about her own experiences and how much she missed her son.

A local activist against violence came to the class and taught my students about trigger locks. A trigger lock is a small device that fits into the trigger space of a gun. It can be locked so that only the person who has the key can unlock and shoot the gun. It is estimated that 15 children in the United States die every day from guns. Trigger locks could prevent all of these deaths. Our visitor organized a program in our community that collected money to purchase trigger locks in bulk.

These trigger locks were distributed at no cost to gun owners in the community.

Working for Change

The children listened carefully. After our visitor left, they agreed that trigger locks could save lives. Then, Sharonda raised her hand and asked a critical question that would drive our work over the next two months: "Ms. Lilly, why don't all guns come with trigger locks?"

I did not have a good answer. After a lengthy discussion we decided that we would write a letter to the gun sellers in our community and encourage them to provide trigger locks with the guns they sell. The class wrote the letter collaboratively and felt strongly about including some of their own thoughts.

Dear Friend,
We are in Ms. Lilly's class at Rosa Parks School. We are six, seven, and eight years old. We are doing a project on violence in our city and we would greatly appreciate it if you could answer a few questions. Please return this paper to us in the enclosed stamped, self-addressed envelope. We really appreciate your help.

1. Why do you sell guns if you know that guns hurt people?
2. Do you realize that people buy guns and sell them to other people? How can we stop this from happening?
3. Why don't you give away free gun locks with the guns you sell and tell people to use the gun locks, not throw them away?

We also have a few comments to share that you might like to address.

- Be careful who you sell guns to because fathers and mothers put bullets in them and kids could pull the trigger and hurt someone.
- Put locks in all guns and throw the keys away.
- Drop guns on the ground and run them over with a garbage truck.
- We would like to shut down your gun shop.

As you can see, the children have some strong opinions. We really value your thoughts.

Thank you,
Cathy Lilly's First Grade Class
Rosa Parks School

We sent this letter to eight gun sellers in our city and received only two responses. The first was a thoughtful response from a man who took the time to answer our questions. He raised issues related to the complexities of people's rights to own guns for hunting, sport, and protection versus the dangers that guns can bring to communities. He also enclosed stickers and other materials from the National Rifle Association and reiterated the rules for children to keep safe from guns. He noted that many guns now come with gun locks and that this is a growing trend in the gun industry. The children listened closely as I read his letter.

The second letter I did not read to the children. In this letter, I was the target of the gun seller's wrath. This man made no attempt to answer the children's questions. Instead he criticized me for spending time on "silly projects" rather than teaching my students "the basics." Clearly this man did not share my notions of critical literacies and how they can be developed in classrooms.

Our project on violence continued with the students surveying their parents about violence and then writing a rap about violence. One of our final projects involved the children writing their own books about violence. Sharonda wrote:

> Violence is not nice.
> It hurts people.
> I hate violence cause violence kills people.
> I don't like violence.
> This is Sharonda saying, "Don't do violence."

A Lesson Learned About Violence

Our unit on confronting violence was an important event in our classroom. Not only was the unit based on a subject of particular interest and concern to my students but it also involved the community in the life of the classroom. Although our letters to local gun store owners were not effective in changing the practices of gun selling in our community, the students participated in a commendable effort to activate change in their community and learned a little bit about the process of working toward change.

At one point during the project, I set up a tape recorder at a table in the back of the classroom. I showed the children how to record and how to stop the tape recorder using the pause button. I had each child go to the back of the room and record his or her own message about violence. Although some children had very little to say and others did little more than giggle into the microphone, Denzon shared a very powerful message:

> Now this is real; I want to tell someone. This one is for real. I think people should stop shooting people with guns. It's not right to shoot people with guns. Just tell the people, make a big, big, big, big sign and tell the people that I say, "Keep the guns to yourselves." If you want a gun you can be a cop. They'll give you a gun but you got to learn how not to shoot people with guns. You got to learn how to make people happy. You got to learn how to not kill anybody with guns. You have to learn that.

Like Roshawn, Denzon was a student who was often difficult in the classroom. He was extremely active and notably distractible. Yet I clearly remember telling his mother about how interested Denzon was in our violence project. As his words indicate, he had strong feelings. This intense interest in school was rarely apparent in his classwork. I wrote in my journal at the time, "Denzon is doing a great job on the violence project, he worked *all* morning."

Perhaps my greatest hope is improbable. Is it possible that the lessons and experiences my students learned during that first grade year could possibly stay with them as they move through adolescence and into adulthood? Will meaningful learning stay with students like Sharonda and Denzon despite the intervening years and the social pressures that sometimes accompany growing up in an urban community? I remain unconvinced, but I do believe that if students were involved in personally relevant issues throughout school, both literacy and school would function differently in students' lives and that we might create a context in which fewer students, like Roshawn, find themselves "stuck in a position." The hope of critical literacy is that students will become empowered to act for change in their own lives and in their communities.

8

Recognizing the Work of Parents

What do students, receptionists, factory workers, bus drivers, construction workers, secretaries, and computer data entry workers have in common? These are some of the jobs held by members of the families of my students. Often urban families are criticized for being on welfare and for not working. When my students explored the jobs held by their family members, we were all impressed by the important contributions their families made.

Although I generally ask the children to choose the topics we study, in some cases outside funding is available. When applying for grants, the procedures for obtaining funding often entail meeting relatively stringent guidelines and tight time frames. That was the case with our exploration of occupations in our community. Small grants became available in our district to support "school-to-work" initiatives. With a little creativity and a bit of flexibility I was able to turn this opportunity into a project that recognized and celebrated the contributions of my students' families.

School-to-work initiatives have been criticized for expecting students to "learn to read and write in particular ways because these ways are valued by business" (Shannon 2002, p. 69). Shannon argues that literacy is treated as a commodity used to the advantage of business and industry. In my project, I proposed to use school-to-work money to help children look inward toward their own families, perhaps disrupting the altruistic discourses on job preparation and replacing them with an emphasis on validating and utilizing resources within the children's families.

Investigating Jobs in Our Community

The plan involved thirty single-use cameras, funds for film processing, and twenty-four aspiring photographers. Once the funding was approved, I described the project to my students and invited them to review and revise the project. The children were excited. In this project, we would first tour the neighborhood around the school to photograph people as they worked in our community. Then, after collaboratively crafting an explanatory letter to their parents, each child would take home a single-use camera with instructions for their parents to take the camera to work and have themselves photographed at their job.

We started out from school one sunny morning heading toward the McDonald's restaurant a block from our school. Armed with one of our single-use cameras, we descended on the community in search of people at work. As we stood at a busy intersection near our school, we found many subjects. A fire truck had stopped in front of the public housing tower on the corner. One firefighter waited in the truck while others completed an inspection of the housing tower. We took the fireman's picture and chatted with him about his job. Seconds later, a police car zipped by as the children snapped a second photo. A passing truck driver became our next target; he blew his horn and waved as he drove through the intersection. The bus stop in front of the housing project provided our next opportunity; we conversed with the driver. While waiting for the light to change, he told us about the stops he makes and the places he goes. Finally, a group of workmen were leaving the housing tower; they waved and smiled as the children snapped their picture.

A couple of days later the film was developed and the children passed the pictures around, busily chatting about the pictures and the people we had met. Of the twenty-four pictures on the roll, the children chose eight to go into a book we wrote about jobs in our community. Over the next week we collaboratively wrote a caption for each of the pictures. Most of the captions simply described the jobs from a child's perspective. For example, the picture of our local McDonald's inspired the following description:

Sometimes I go to McDonald's. The people at McDonald's are nice to us because they give us food. They cook the food. Hamburgers are the best.

However, other pictures elicited writing that revealed sentiments I had found foreign when I first started teaching at Rosa Parks School:

Some people hate cops because they are mean. They take us to jail and we get out in a long time. The police is looking for the bad guys to go away because it is the way of the time.

This statement is particularly interesting in the ways that it positions the children through the use of the words "us" and "we." Although the quote begins by qualifying that the statement refers only to "some people," the children do not describe the police as arresting some people; the children wrote, "they take *us* to jail." Obviously six-year-olds do not go to jail, however, the children in my class clearly positioned themselves as members of a community who are often the recipients of the police officers' actions.

When I first started teaching in the city, my first reaction would have been to attempt to convince my students that police are not really bad and that they are working to keep people safe. But as I have gained more experience as a city teacher, I have come to understand that my reality may not reflect the reality of my students and their families. In some cases, the parents I have interviewed have helped me to understand this perspective about the police. One late spring evening, Ms. Rodriguez told me a horrifying story about how her older son was arrested for no reason:

MS. RODRIGUEZ: I fear the gangs too but I don't fear [them] as much as I fear the police.
CL: Really.
MS. RODRIGUEZ: With my sons, I fear the police more than anything because they get stopped for no apparent reason. Leon had on a book bag and they stopped Leon.
CL: Walking?
MS. RODRIGUEZ: Yeah, he was right at the . . .

CL: He was just walking down the street?

MS. RODRIGUEZ: Yeah he was at the corner store. I sent Jared to the store for me and Leon went too, and Leon went to the store and when Jared come out the store, the cops got his brother on the wall because he looked suspicious with a book bag. So when Jared asked him what was going on, they told him to move and then that night they end up arresting him, so I had to go down to the police station to bail my son out. It is more of the police that I fear with my kids. It is not the gangs and it is not really the people in the street. It is the police. When they walk out this door, my fear is that I am going to get a phone call that my son is either downtown or they accidentally shot my son or something. That's my worst fear. Mistaking him for somebody else. . . . I think being young and black and they figured most young black people they figure are either out there selling drugs or doing drugs and they think because you live in the ghetto . . . you got to act like the ghetto. But that's not true.

Having known Ms. Rodriguez and her older children for many years, I had come to know her sons as responsible and hardworking students who generally earn good grades and often balance part-time jobs with school. As far as I know they have never been in any trouble with the law. Even issues as simple as learning about community helpers are complicated by race and residence in an poor urban community.

Investigating Jobs in the Students' Families

When the day came for each of the children to take home their own single-use cameras, the children were very excited. We crafted a note to their parents explaining the project and then brainstormed a list of possible subjects to photograph. As we drafted the letter, several issues arose that I had not anticipated. Malisa raised her hand and asked, "What do we do if our mom or dad doesn't have a job?" Together we brainstormed some alternatives for children in this situation. We noted that children could ask an extended family member to help them with the project.

Grandparents, aunts, uncles, and older siblings were among the possibilities. We also spoke at length about the work parents did in the home and discussed the importance of childcare and housework. Children could photograph people, including themselves, working at home.

Another important issue was raised when Michael asked, "What should I do if my parents don't live together and they both work?" A class member quickly proposed a solution: "Have both parents take the camera to work." This is just what Michael did. By the time we finished our discussion, we agreed that in addition to documenting people's jobs that pictures of family members were also important; the children voiced a strong interest in taking pictures of the important people in their lives. Obviously, my original conception of the project had been too narrow. I had not viewed the task from the children's perspective and failed to consider some of its complexities. This experience again demonstrated the importance of listening to children and including their perspectives when planning projects. Together we reached a collaborative agreement concerning the parameters of the project. We agreed that different children would be using their cameras in different ways. We made a list of things that could be photographed:

> Take a picture of yourself.
>
> Take a picture of your brothers and sisters.
>
> Take a picture of your parents.
>
> Take pictures of your house.
>
> Take pictures of where your parents, aunts, uncles, brothers, and/or sisters work.
>
> Take a picture of your parents, aunts, uncles, brothers and/or sisters at work.
>
> Take pictures of people working in your home.

All of the children returned their cameras to school. As they brought in their cameras, I had the film developed. There were some surprises when I viewed the developed photographs. Shandra was one of the first students to return her camera to school. She brought it back the day after taking it home. I praised her for her diligence but soon realized how she managed to complete the task so quickly. When the film was developed, it was clear that Shandra's camera ran out of film before she reached home. All twenty-four pictures were taken of people on the school bus. That roll of film supported Shandra's reputation for impulsivity among the teachers at our school. Shandra was embarrassed when I showed her the pictures. My first reaction was frustration and annoyance, but that soon passed. Although Shandra's pictures did not meet the requirements of the assignment, like the other kids she wrote a book based on the pictures she had taken. The caption under a photograph of a young boy read, "I saw a boy and then I just took a picture." A shot of a very stern-faced bus driver looking directly at the camera read, "That bus driver is watching somebody."

Although a few children took pictures only of their families, most did include photographs of their parents at work. Gayden's book opens with pictures of Gayden and his family. His father works on an assembly line where they make televsions. Gayden's father included pictures of himself using a computer, driving a forklift, and standing beside his colleagues next to boxes of completed televisions.

Doneeta's book also opens with pictures of her family. The second page shows Doneeta receiving a big hug from her grandmother. The next few pages present Doneeta's grandmother as she goes through her day as a school bus driver (see Figure 8–1). The children were fascinated

Figure 8–1 Doneeta's picture shows her grandmother driving her bus.

with Doneeta's pictures and account. Although many of them ride the bus every day, they did not know what bus drivers do when they are not actually driving the bus. The office that coordinates routes and distributes keys was fascinating to the children. A wall covered with bus keys and the parking lot full of buses brought a new perspective to the children's everyday experiences.

Perhaps the most interesting book to the children was about McKenzie's mother, who directs traffic at road construction sites (see Figure 8–2). In addition to inspiring a lengthy conversation about the jobs that women can hold, McKenzie's mother had been careful to take pictures of each step in the road construction process—from digging up the old asphalt to smoothing out the new road. The children learned about the entire process.

After the children viewed their pictures, wrote about them, and made books, we invited the adults to visit our classroom. Several relatives were able to attend. The children read their books to the class. They introduced their relatives, and classmates were invited to ask questions about the visitors' occupations.

Figure 8–2 McKenzie's mother directs traffic at the construction site.

Lessons Learned About Families

This project accomplished several things. First, it explored a topic that was personally significant to the children. Whether their book was about their parents' jobs, their families, or their ride home on the school bus, it was a relevant writing opportunity. Second, by collecting these pictures and valuing them at school, we dignified the work of the parents. We discussed the important roles of receptionists, factory workers, bus drivers, construction workers, and secretaries. We even tried to envision a world without these people. Finally, the project brought parents and other family members into the classroom to share their knowledge and expertise. When schools and teachers recognize the abilities and contributions of the parents of their students, new relationships begin to emerge that acknowledge and celebrate what parents have to offer.

9

A School-Wide Project:
Learning About Lead Poisoning

"Ms. Lilly, we found lead on the wall!" exclaimed one of my excited six-year-old students. I was completely taken aback. "Where? Let me see that test strip. There can't be lead here; this school was renovated just a few years ago," I replied hastily. With amazement I looked down at the bright pink test strip. That afternoon, a colleague and I thoroughly checked our classroom walls for the presence of lead. It was everywhere, especially in places where the new paint was chipped.

As a teacher in an urban community, I am very familiar with the effects that lead poisoning can have on the lives of my students and their family members. It is not unusual to refer a child to the district's committee on special education and then learn that the child has a history of high lead. Lead poisoning is a very real problem in the community where I teach. Most of my students reside in older homes that have been converted into apartments. Often these rental properties are not well maintained by landlords, and there is no systematic inspection for lead paint in rental properties in our city. Most families become aware of lead hazards only after a child has been poisoned.

Nationally, public health officials have declared lead the number one environmental hazard to American children (National Institute of Environmental Health Services 1997). Children under the age of seven are the most at-risk for lead poisoning, with sustained lead exposure in childhood being associated with lowered IQs, lowered rates of high school graduation, and increased delinquency rates (Brooks 2000).

Although the sale of lead paint in America was banned in 1977, a 1986 Environmental Protection Agency report stated that 52 percent of homes in the United States contain lead paint (National Institute of Environmental Health Services 1997). Lead paint is also found in soil and lead pipe solder.

While most of the projects described in this book were chosen and planned by my students, this project required outside funding; I selected the topic. The grant application process occurred months before the start of the project, and the children whom I taught while I was writing the grant were not the same children who would be in my class during the implementation of the project. However, as with the occupations unit, I used my knowledge about the community and my experiences with my students and their families to select a project that I suspected my students would find relevant. Our lead project was supported by a $10,000 Toyota Tapestry Grant (sponsored by Toyota Motor Sales, Inc., and administered by the National Science Teachers Association).

Part of the grant application process involved making connections with local organizations to support our efforts. I contacted our local health department and enthusiastically described my vision for a hands-on project in which children could actually test their school and their homes for lead paint. My enthusiasm was met with a poignant pause from the director of the lead poisoning department. He tried to convince me that perhaps it would be better to simply show the children a filmstrip or to borrow some of the curriculum materials that were available. After all, what would happen if families did find lead? What if they all called the health department in panic? He explained that there are very limited funds available for lead removal in our community. Despite his reservations, he agreed to sign off on the grant.

Learning About the Dangers of Lead

Our lead poisoning project was a school-wide initiative that involved children from kindergarten through grade five. During the first part of the project, my colleagues and I created a series of presentations for students. For children in grades one and two, teachers used an overhead projector to share a children's story provided by the New York State Health Department about ways to stay safe from lead. Teachers role-played going to the doctor for a blood test and being checked for lead.

Older children were shown a video about the dangers of lead and discussed what they had seen. Throughout these presentations lead was portrayed as a very dangerous substance that should be avoided by all children. The children learned that lead affects children's brains and that young children are particularly susceptible to lead poisoning.

We shared with our students the basic rules for lead safety such as regular hand-washing and reminders not to put things in their mouths. Older children were provided with information to share with their parents about keeping their homes lead-safe; they learned the importance of wet-mopping floors where children play and letting the water run for a couple minutes each morning before using it for baby formula or food preparation.

Particular attention was granted to the role older children could play in helping their younger brothers and sisters stay safe from lead. Jordan, a first grader, came to school one day reporting with pride that he had told his younger sister to stay away from the peeling paint in his apartment. Sandra, another first grader, read her sisters a storybook about lead provided by the health department; she reported, "Don't worry, Ms. Lilly. They know all about lead, but I'd still better keep an eye on them!"

Staff presentations were followed by visits from representatives from the local health department and a nearby health center. The visitor from the health department brought our youngest children rubber ducks and small bars of soap to remind children of the importance of washing their hands. A local health center volunteer spoke with older students about how lead affects children's growing bodies. Students learned how lead can slow children's physical and intellectual growth. Lead is stored in bone marrow and can interfere with red blood cell production. In addition, lead can cause kidney damage, hearing defects, and even death.

Our First Family Event

Through these presentations, students became well informed about the presence and dangers of lead in our community. Teachers continued to explore the dangers of lead poisoning in their classrooms. Fifth grade students wrote essays about the dangers of lead poisoning. Students in second and third grade classes composed rap songs about lead. First grade students wrote letters to their parents and pediatricians asking them to make sure that children are tested for lead poisoning. Meg wrote:

> dar doktr chak us four lead.
> *Dear doctor, check us for lead.*

Classes from across the school created songs, skits, and poems for a professionally edited video funded by our Toyota Tapestry Grant. This video along with posters made by every student in the school and student writing were shared with parents at a family night in November (see Figure 9–1). Rodney, a student in my first grade class, wrote and illustrated this message:

> Lead is Dns Ksuzz its se. Lead Mac you hD to Thei.
> *Lead is dangerous 'cause it's poison. Lead makes you hard to think.*

Meg wrote about how in Europe they stopped making lead paint in the 1920s.

> In Europe They stopd making Lead. in the USA They Keepd on making Lead Pant.
> *In Europe they stopped making lead. In the USA they kept on making lead paint.*

Figure 9–1 Charles' picture shows the production of lead paint. His caption reads, "When the USA sold lead they kept on making more money."

Over 200 people attended this informational event and enjoyed a family pizza dinner.

Testing, Testing, Testing

We began the second half of the project in January. Test kits were distributed to each teacher, and students tested their classrooms and other places in our school for lead (see Figure 9–2). The lead test kits were very simple to use. The students were told to clean the targeted spot with soap and water. The test strip was then placed on the target spot and a drop of vinegar was applied to the oval window on the test strip. The strips were left in place for five minutes. After five minutes the test strip was removed and the color was compared with the guide on the front of the test strip package. Green and gray pigments indicated that lead was not present while pink indicated the presence of lead.

Our school was built in 1911; the building had been abandoned for five years. In preparation for it reopening in 1993, the building was entirely renovated and reopened as a sparkling new elementary school.

Figure 9–2 *Charles prepares to test a paint sample; he will wear protective gloves and safety glasses.*

Although only seven years had passed since the school was reopened, there were many places where the paint was chipped. To our surprise students in every classroom found lead. Not only was lead paint lurking beneath the recent layers of paint, but it was also on floors and on the painted sides of some desks. Hallway floors and floor boards consistently tested positive for lead. The bus gate in front of the school, from which long strips of yellow paint peeled off in my hand, tested positive for lead.

Students also checked their school yard for the presence of lead (see Figure 9–3). Soil samples from various places in our school yard were collected in September by first grade students; in the northeast part of the country, we might not be able to collect soil samples from under the snow during the winter months. These samples were bagged and coded on a map of the school yard. Lead soil kits were used to detect lead in the soil. This testing process involved placing soil samples in a vial and mixing them with a small amount of vinegar. Test strips were then dipped into the mixture. After waiting five minutes, the color of the test strip indicated the presence or absence of lead. Of the eighteen soil samples students collected, thirteen tested positive for lead. Fortunately, the fresh soil mixed with wood chips beneath our new playground was lead-free.

Figure 9–3 Rodney and Marisa take soil samples from the school yard.

While the students were quite concerned about the presence of lead in their classrooms and in the school yard, we reminded them of ways they could stay safe. We discussed the fact that the floors were testing positive due to lead being tracked into classrooms from the school yard. The walls were testing positive due to old layers of lead paint. Safety guidelines such as hand-washing, staying away from peeling paint, and keeping things out of their mouths were reviewed.

Each classroom was surveyed to identify places where paint was chipped. Every teacher was asked to have the students identify places in their classroom where the paint was chipping, fill out a reporting form, and return their findings to the Lead Project Planning Committee. The results of this investigation were shared with the maintenance staff from our district along with a letter written by a team of fifth grade students asking them to repair chipped paint in our building.

Focusing on Children's Homes

For the final activity of the project, all 300 students at my school were invited to take a lead test kit home to test their homes for lead. Over 125 kits were sent home. Although the children seemed excited as they took the kits home, I was disappointed in the low return rate of the home lead testing forms. Even after accounting for the forgetfulness of students, a very small proportion of the students who took test kits home returned their results to school. A woman who works in the lead program at a local health clinic described similar problems with getting parents to report to the health center whether or not they were aware of the presence of lead in their homes. She explained that parents are often reluctant to let us know when they find lead in their homes. They know that they should remove the lead but few can afford the costs of lead abatement. They worry about having to find another apartment on a limited budget. Phone calls from parents and comments from children confirmed these fears. One parent called to apologize for not returning her son's lead testing form; she explained that she felt uncomfortable sharing the results with the school. Other children came to me and said that their parents told them that they couldn't bring the papers back. Understandably, parents in low-income communities are often reluctant to divulge sensitive information to local institutions, including schools, for fear of possible consequences.

The results of the home lead tests that were returned to school were posted in our main hallway. Positive occurrences of lead were much higher than the fifty-two percent reported nationally. Eighty-seven percent of the forms returned to my school were positive. While some parents were justly concerned about the presence of lead in their homes, prior to testing both the children and their parents were introduced to measures that can be taken to prevent lead from hurting children and the dangers that lead can have for young children. Many children spoke with me over the course of the project. "Ms. Lilly, I found lead in my bedroom." "Ms. Lilly, my mom moved my sister's crib because there is lead paint by her window." "Ms. Lilly, I told my brother to not touch the walls upstairs because there is lead." Although awareness is only the beginning, it can help families to remain safe.

A Lesson Shared with Families

In the spring, we again invited parents to our school to share the results of our research. We had found lead in our school, in the school yard, and in the homes of children and staff members. Lynette, a fifth grade student, stood beside me with a nervous smile on her face and confided, "I don't know what to say." "Don't worry," I told her, "just do it the way we practiced." She self-consciously walked up to the microphone. By her second sentence she was enthusiastic. "The red dots represent places where there is lead. As you can see there's *a lot* of red," reported Lynette as she pointed to the red dots on a floor plan of the school and then on an enlarged map of the city that showed where lead had been found in students' homes.

Again, representatives from the county health department and a local health center were available to answer questions and provide advice. The event was met with rave reviews from parents who wanted to know why all schools were not making children and parents aware of the dangers of lead in their communities.

Science is not just the stuff of laboratories. Science is about people's lives. Through our critical literacy project our students had a wonderful opportunity to learn about one way science can address real issues in their lives.

10

Paying and Paying Back: Employing Critical Literacy in the Humanities to Examine the Warp and Woof of Democracy

By Todd Lilly, Teacher of Secondary Language Arts

"Who paid for you?"

It was obvious that the speaker had succeeded in getting the students' attention. They sat in their caps and gowns listening intently as the speaker repeated the question. "Who paid for you?" This was clearly a new idea for the students. Evidently, no one had given much thought to the notion that a free education isn't free. The speaker wasn't finished: "And how are you going to pay back?"

Good questions—questions that strike to the core of our concept of democracy. The first question exposes the myth that education is a matter of individual engagement. If education is free, then students, teachers, parents, and the whole community are absolved of any responsible investment. But if we all are made to face the true costs—the costs in money, in time, in emotional investment—then we are all accountable, and the second question becomes worthy of deliberation.

The Thirty-Year Mortgage

My wife and I are products of public school districts that were funded by the residents of the municipalities in which the boundaries of those districts lie. Some of those residents had children; some did not. Some of those residents had incomes substantially higher than our parents; some just the opposite. The state in which we lived also invested heavily in our public school districts, and so did the federal government, which means that people from all walks of life, from all income levels, from all creeds and races had a stake in paying for our educations. Furthermore, we both studied and received our teaching certificates at state colleges, and both of us finished our teacher training at public schools: mine in an urban high school, my wife's in a suburban setting. Who paid? Lots of people, from the homeowners rich and small to the buyers of lottery tickets in liquor stores all across the state.

After a couple years in city schools, I obtained my present job in the suburbs, while my wife taught a couple years in the suburbs and ended up with her current job in a large city school district. Together, we can afford a comfortable life. We're happy, as are so many who have flowed from suburban settings through public institutions into adult lives as full-fledged participants in American society. The vast majority of the students from the suburban high school where I work, those students who listened so intently to the prodding speaker at their graduation ceremony, are following those same waters, a river whose current will sweep most of them and their peers across the country into the mainstream of middle-class America. Most—but not all.

I grew up in a community that was very similar to the one in which I now teach: very white, very middle class, very dedicated to the American Dream that convinced us all that we could be whatever we wanted to become. Many of my peers went to college; most of the others got jobs in local industries. Several started their own businesses. I do not recall ever doubting the assumptions we all had for our own successes.

I attended my thirtieth high school reunion recently. There were very few surprises. We had virtually all ended up in white, middle-class suburbs. The reunion took place in a party house in our hometown where many of our wedding receptions have been held over the years. At the door we signed in and filled out our name cards, which the reunion committee had coordinated with our twelfth grade yearbook picture. As I signed the registration book, the woman at the desk looked up at me and blurted, "Are you a teacher? You have my son Jimmy in one of your classes." In fact, I've had several of my classmates' children as students. It occurred to me that each of us attending that reunion was paying back the investments our parents' generation bestowed on us. We became middle-class citizens who hold jobs, pay taxes, obey laws, and raise children who do likewise. It is an assumption we make for all Americans, but in doing so, we perpetuate a myth.

High Risk Futures

My awakening occurred when I was in my early twenties and the fates decided that I was to complete my student teaching assignment in a large, urban high school. After I had been there for two weeks my supervising teacher was hospitalized for an acute ulcer and I was left to fend for myself. For the first time in my life I was submerged in a culture that was clearly not my own. The river that had swept me through grade school and then on through college was barely a trickle running through this school. These kids looked different, their language was difficult to understand, and they certainly weren't listening to Eric Clapton and the Doobie Brothers. It was a fascinating world where kids spoke in loud voices and formed close bonds and allegiances. These were kids who lived very much for the moment, with energy that exploded in the now without much momentum to carry them into the future. Never had I seen such energy. Groups of girls would spontaneously break out in song. A fight could erupt from nowhere within seconds. Three girls, two of whom were black and the other white, named themselves "The Oreo Cookie" and paraded through the halls arm-in-arm. Kids who could assault you with their eyes would come in on Monday morning talking about how they spent all yesterday in church.

These kids knew who they were and where they came from, and where they came from had little to do with the faces in their history books. I remember students boasting of how much Native American blood was coursing through their veins. And occasionally, perhaps out of sympathy to my awkwardness, someone would confide to me of a white relative or would point out someone in the class who had a white relative. One student claimed to be a close relative of William Warfield. I was doubtful. "You mean *the* William Warfield? The *Porgy and Bess* William Warfield?" I asked. He opened his wallet and showed me a picture of the two of them together. He knew who he was. Then there was Henry. Halfway through the semester the school realized that both of Henry's parents were in jail, and nobody was minding Henry. So where was Henry living? It turned out that he had made a little nest for himself in an unused garage in the back of a house a couple blocks from the school. At fifteen years old, Henry had a pride that wasn't going to allow himself to be beholden to anyone merely because of where he came from.

In the city, "normal" classroom protocols were chaotic and anything but routine. We never conducted a planned fire drill. Someone would always pull the alarm and we could hear the fire trucks approaching the building as we descended the stairs. There was no such thing as a neat grade book. Class rosters would change weekly as kids moved from one house to another around the city. I discovered that large city school districts rarely expel students. They merely transfer incorrigible pupils from one city school to another to become someone else's problem. I quickly learned to be wary of newcomers.

My saving grace was that somewhere in my genetic code I shared with these kids a comic wit. I discovered quite naturally that the same character trait that used to drive my high school English teacher crazy could be a valuable asset in classroom management. They made assumptions about me just as I had made assumptions about them. The game was that we could keep each other off guard by constantly challenging those assumptions. When a student once threatened to get his lawyer after me when I refused to allow him to use the facilities during a test, I opened my wallet and handed him my lawyer's card and told him to have his lawyer get in touch with my lawyer and maybe they could work something out. The class snickered, I smiled, the student with the bladder condition smiled, and we all survived.

But I eventually discovered that the best "games" were the ones that positioned the students and me on the same side of the court instead of pitting us against each other. I recall a problem with a class that I had immediately after lunch. The students were always late getting to class, and I assumed they were merely taking advantage of me. So I did what any normal teacher would do: I threatened them with detention. The response was predictable. They complained it wasn't their fault, and they had no intention of showing up for detention. They argued that the cafeteria staff was consistently late in opening the food lines at the beginning of the lunch period, which didn't give the kids enough time to eat. It sounded like a reasonable excuse to me and I told them so. This opened a floodgate. They had other issues with the school ranging from homeroom procedures to locker searches by school security to crowd control at varsity basketball games.

The next day I showed up with a stack of ditto masters. We took the top sheets off the ditto masters and replaced them with lined notebook paper on which the kids could write more legibly. The class broke into groups and each group took a different bothersome issue involving school procedures. We talked about what we wanted to achieve and wording that would help us attain a favorable outcome. We also talked about wording that might be too inflammatory. We arranged and conducted interviews. I remember passing one of the school administrators in the hallway and briefly informing him of what we were up to. I don't recall his response, except I know he didn't exactly say no. Within a few days we had a crude journal printed up ready to be distributed during lunch. We actually watched people reading the articles. We heard them talking about our articles. The students were excited; they weren't exactly dancing in the halls, but it sure beat writing about how Johnny Tremain changed from the beginning of the novel to the end. The principal wrote us a note explaining that the problem with the food lines in the lunchroom was caused when a supervisor left for another job. He promised that a new supervisor had been hired and would be starting work immediately.

We also received a threatening letter from the "official" school newspaper accusing us of "unsanctioned competition." We were not even aware that there was an official school newspaper. We put out a few more issues and then the official editor of the official newspaper visited our class to officially scold us in person. We stood our ground. Shortly thereafter we abandoned our little critical literacy project; it had run its course. Students still came late to class, but the class had changed. My wife and I were expecting our first child at the time, and I discovered that there was a secret pool worth several dollars to the class member who could most accurately guess the precise moment our child was to be born. At the end of the year two girls in the class offered their phone numbers in case I needed their baby-sitting services.

Subsequently, I accepted a temporary position in the district but soon discovered that one of the biggest dilemmas I faced working in the city was that I would be laid off at the end of each school year. I could not be assured of employment literally until the Labor Day weekend merely because the district had no idea what the actual enrollment would be for the following year. With a family to support, I found this unacceptable. After two years in the city I was hired in a suburban district whose superintendent assured me that if I had what it took to survive in the city, I would certainly succeed in the suburbs. I owe much to the faculty, staff, students, and taxpayers of the city school district—not only for changing my life but also, in fact, for defining it.

Refinancing

In the course of my tenure with the suburban district where I now work, I have had the opportunity to teach English at every grade level between seven and twelve. Several years ago I happened to be teaching Charles Dickens' *A Christmas Carol* to ninth graders. This is a book that gets right to the heart of the matter. "Mankind was my business." *"How are you going to pay back?"* "What can we put you down for?" One year just before Christmas, which was typically when my classes would be in the midst of Dickens' London, I called a family meeting to discuss our despicable lack of charitable giving for the year. We certainly hadn't tithed, not even half a tithe, not even a quarter. It seemed like a good Rockwellian type of thing to do: to have the family discuss a few possibilities in a democratic manner and vote on a plan regarding how to spend Mom and Dad's money. Surely, we could come up with a charity or two that could use some extra capital. Our kids dismissed the idea with a contemptuous roll of the eyes and disappeared into their rooms. So, determined to allay my guilt by means of a modest check or two delivered to some desperate mission where people sat around like Bob Cratchit with their bare fingers sticking out the ends of their gloves, I took my case to a more captive audience—my ninth graders. I explained to them how it is in the American psyche to be generous and that I was not doing anything that their parents and neighbors didn't do: sharing our good fortunes with those in need. I assured them that I wasn't asking them for money; all I wanted was their honest, sincere ideas about what charitable establishments I should assist with a meager donation. I asked each student to think about what organization my family and I should support and why, and then write a paper persuading the class and me that the chosen charity should, indeed, be funded. Papers were to be typed and submitted anonymously and then shipped off to another class for consideration. This was not to be a popularity contest. Students were forewarned that there would be a selection process, and not all of their choices would be funded. They were assured that selected papers would be signed by the writer and sent on to the named charity along with my check.

Each class was guaranteed a limited number of modest checks so that students who were serious would need to be mindful of all the techniques of good, persuasive writing. Not all but most of the students quickly came up with an idea and went right to work. Many of the kids actually made phone calls to institutions to find out how much money they received during a typical year and where it all went. More than a few of these establishments offered to send representatives to the school to talk to the kids. We set a strict due date for the papers, refusing to consider papers that came in late. I remember one father running down a hallway with his ill daughter's paper in hand, making sure it got in under the wire. I read the opening lines as I walked to class: "It is an unfortunate custom in South Korea for mothers of newborns who cannot afford the child's upkeep to abandon the baby in the doorway of a police station. Fifteen years ago, I was found in a box in front of just such a police station in Seoul." The girl who wrote this is now studying to become an English teacher.

The papers from each class were carefully collected and delivered to students in another class, who worked in groups to choose what they perceived to be the best papers. We played a version of "pass the trash" in which each group would read a set of compositions, quickly choose the best, and then discard the rest to the next group. The next group would then decide whether any of the previous group's discarded papers were better than the one they had kept from their previous batch. After about twenty minutes all of the papers had been thoroughly circulated and each group had what we called a "keeper." I collected the keepers. Each group was required to write a note on a 5 × 7 index card to the writer of each unselected contribution explaining why his or her paper was not selected as a keeper. All of the students whose papers were selected were invited to an after-school reception where each of them read his or her paper and received editing suggestions from the group. Although a donation was sent to each of the charities named in the keeper papers, the students voted for two of the keeper papers whose named charitable institutions would receive a more substantial donation.

Many of the rejected papers were predictable. One boy wanted money for his Saturday morning bowling team. Many chose national or even international organizations merely because of their name recognition. Some of these suburban kids seemed to live charmed lives with no personal knowledge of or connection to places of charity. But then there were the others that still haunt me years later.

For instance, one boy wrote of his little brother, who was born with a degenerative birth defect. He related how a little yellow school bus would come every morning to take his brother to a special daycare facility and then return him home in the afternoon. They had a little dog who would faithfully wait by the window each day until the brother was safely returned. Then one day the yellow bus didn't need to stop at their house anymore, but the dog still waited at the window every day for months, waiting for the little boy to return. I sent the letter with my enclosed check to the daycare institution. A few weeks later I received a note from a worker there who wrote of how much she and her coworkers missed the little boy and were deeply saddened at his passing. I was humbled to consider how some people pay back with their whole lives rather than simply writing a check.

Principle and Interest

This assignment facilitated real, meaningful dialogue in the class and broached subjects, often taboo subjects, that were completely unknown to some students and deeply, sometimes tragically known to others. We got to know people on different levels that had previously remained unexamined. We sometimes even talked about what was appropriate to share and what might be more respectfully left unsaid. I have been guilty of assigning dozens of purely "exercise" compositions in my career, but clearly writing can go beyond the superficial. One girl very delicately wrote of her sister's hospitalization for mental illness, a condition that is unjustly imbued with a myriad of false assumptions.

> My sister, Mary, has been in the hospital for six months now. She hasn't gone places with friends or danced for a long time. She spent her sixteenth birthday in her hospital room. Without her home, I

have a lot of time to think of how much I really miss her. It occurs to me that her life is going down the drain while I go on every day with my normal one. I take for granted how good my life is, schoolwork and all. Please realize that she would switch with me in a second; but she can't—she isn't able to. Sometimes I talk to her on the telephone, but she is changed. . . . It scares me to think that she may never be the same Mary that I once knew.

This letter was sent with a check to a local children's hospital. A few weeks later I received a personal letter from the director of the hospital inviting me to come and tour the facility as his guest.

There is no question that this assignment greatly enriched my relationship not only with my students but also with their parents. Although I told my classes that I was only doing what their parents did privately and although I requested that they keep the assignment as private as possible, the project clearly instilled a different sense of community involving students, parents, a few of my colleagues who knew of the assignment, certain members of the community who had ties to any of the charitable organizations affected by the assignment, myself, and even my wife. For my wife and me it was payback time. We are well aware that it is the parents of these students and the community at large who contribute to our well-being.

One of the aspects of this project that I found extremely hopeful was that it often transcended the urban-suburban divide. This, perhaps, is what my wife had in mind when she asked me to write this chapter for her book. The suburb in which I teach is referred to as an "inner ring" suburb, meaning it is an older community at the fringe of the city where most of the lot sizes are a third of an acre or less. In fact, some of my students live only a few blocks away from the students my wife writes about in her accounts recorded in this book. As in many cities, a wide commuter expressway carved between the two communities offers an effective buffer between the haves and the have-nots. Many of my students have never ventured through the streets on the other side of the divide, not even with their parents. A few of the older students at my school hazard across solely to conduct illicit transactions at infamous street corners. One of my student's parents once adamantly refused to allow her son to attend a school theater project at a city school just blocks from her home, literally fearing her fifteen-year-old would never return alive.

One respected member of the suburban community summed up his defense of the lack of meaningful dialogue across the divide: "I can't stand their music, and they don't like mine. So I don't visit their churches and they don't come to mine. That's just the way it is."

Yet, because of the writings of students in my classes, my wife and I have contributed to urban outreach ministries that provide basic necessities, counseling, and even homework assistance to people, regardless of race or religion, who feel "life is going down the drain." Students have often shared with the class their personal experiences with these ministries and other urban empowerment programs where false assumptions have been reconciled with face-to-face encounters, just as mine had years ago. Wesley's paper illustrates one of those encounters:

> When my mom called me over to help a lady skate around the rink a couple of times at the West Avenue Family Resource Center's annual ice-skating party, I cursed under my breath and rolled my eyes into the back of my head. I figured it would be just another boring skate around the rink at 2 mph with an occasional fall that I was expected to break. We were introduced to each other and sent on our way outside to the arctic weather.
>
> As Sharon and I took baby steps onto the frozen rink, I noticed that she had jeans with holes in the knees and lacked a hat and gloves. The merciless wind that never used to faze me now went straight to the bone.
>
> I thought to myself: "This won't take five minutes. She'll be back inside with hot chocolate as soon as we walk out to the ice." But as the minutes slipped by, her smile seemed to grow wider and wider. I became colder and colder.
>
> I began to wonder, why doesn't she have a practical jacket? Is it because her parents can't afford it? We continued to skate around the rink, and I was glad she was having fun, but every time we went around, I was sure she would give in and take shelter in the warm, cozy building that called to me every time we passed.
>
> Later, I learned that Sharon had been on her own since age 13 and was a mother at 15. She also didn't have a high school diploma. And with four kids now, welfare will most likely be a part of the rest of her life.
>
> Out of nowhere it hit me! I know why she enjoyed it so much—it was because she had been robbed of her own childhood. Sharon never knew what it was like to have fun because she had to grow up

so fast. This poverty-stricken family needs as much help as it can get, and that's where the West Avenue Family Resource Center comes in. Sharon was referred to them by social services because her children were considered at risk.

The center was founded in September 1981 to strengthen and support families, to reduce isolation, and to provide a nurturing atmosphere with a range of educational, social and supportive services in a neighborhood setting. The center is a part of a nationwide family support movement that includes five local centers, recently united in a Family Resource Center network. West Avenue is one of the oldest centers and is considered the model for other centers regionally.

In spite of tough economic struggles, many of the original staff have remained and remain dedicated and committed to the center's mission. Along with services of parent education, like skills classes, and the Young Adult Mothers program, Sharon has gained acceptance, respect, affection and support from the employees who make up the family that she doesn't have.

The West Avenue Family Resource Center's success is dependent on donations, grants, volunteers, and staff. Without the center's help, Sharon might have lost her children to foster care and could be in a worse situation. I believe it is our responsibility to help the less fortunate help themselves. Sharon deserves this extra chance to put her life back on track.

Lessons Learned About Meaningful Investments

"Who paid for you? How are you going to pay back?" These two questions just might be the warp and woof of our democratic fabric, and as such, they deserve a central prominence in the discourse of our humanities curricula. Who pays the tab? Financially, emotionally, intellectually, with life-stained lives; we all do. So many facets of investing and paying back can be investigated in order to challenge our traditional "exercise" approaches to reading, writing, and living. American-style democracy is an exciting, dynamic, all-inclusive experiment that requires active minds to sift through the assumptions of who pays and how each of us pays back. We needn't wait until graduation to ask the good questions.

REFLECTION

This book is full of questions. I began by asking questions of my readers. In my own research, I asked my students and their parents many questions. During the critical literacy projects that occurred in my classroom, and in my husband's classroom, our students pursued their own questions. Yet with all of these questions being asked and answered, I continue to discover still more questions and realize that the remaining questions are perhaps the most critical and yet most daunting.

How can we disrupt dominant ways of thinking to help teachers, administrators, policy makers, politicians, and the general public rethink assumptions that are part of the fabric of American culture? How can we move beyond these assumptions to begin to create a "third space" where teachers, students, parents, and communities can find ways to use the myriad resources we collectively possess to provide educational experiences for children that invite and extend rather than evaluate and deny? How can we design classroom learning experiences that recognize and build on the linguistic and literacy knowledge that children and their families possess? I hope this book is an initial step in beginning to crack the grip of dominance, denial, and dismissal.

Appendix
Methodology of the Teacher Research Study

For eight years I taught at Rosa Parks Elementary School; it is a large, crowded school (850 students) located in the poorest neighborhood of a mid-sized Northeastern city. Ninety-seven percent of the children at this school qualify for free or reduced lunches. Before coming to Rosa Parks School, I taught in a nearby suburban school district. The change was difficult, and my first years at Rosa Parks were tumultuous. I struggled with defining my role as a white teacher of African American and Hispanic children. My inexperience contributed to problems within the classroom and difficulties managing the maze of bureaucratic procedures outside of the classroom that characterize teaching in a large urban district. I often wondered if I was the best-qualified person to be teaching my students.

The insights described in this book are part of a larger teacher-researcher study that became my doctoral dissertation and eventually a book (Compton-Lilly 2003). To explore the concepts about reading held by urban first grade students and their parents, I randomly selected and interviewed ten of my first grade students and their parents about reading and schooling. All interviews were audiotaped and transcribed in full with the exception of clearly off-topic comments. These interviews along with student portfolios, transcriptions of class discussions, and field notes were analyzed to identify themes and issues that captured families' conceptions about reading.

The families who participated in my research study were primarily African American, Puerto Rican, and biracial. However, these demographics do not begin to capture the variety of personalities, interests,

abilities, and struggles that characterize the individual students in my class. Their parents too represent a broad range of individuals. Among the parents I interviewed were parents who were unemployed as well as parents who had steady jobs. Some parents were on welfare; others had not been on welfare since they were children. One parent had earned an Associates degree; other parents had not graduated from high school. The parents of children in my class grew up in cities, were raised in the South, lived in suburban communities, and were raised in small rural towns.

During the 1997–98 school year, I started taking field notes during the days that led up to the opening of school. Our school had been placed on a list of low-performing schools by the State Education Department, and the days before the children arrived were full of meetings and school improvement inservice sessions. Several of these focused on the new basal reading series we were piloting.

As the children arrived later that week, I recorded descriptions of the classroom and the children daily. My intent was to focus on concepts about reading that were held by my students and their families. However, as I review the field notes I kept during that school year, in addition to comments about children and their literacy practices, I find many references to the ongoing disputes within the school as teachers, administrators, and staff developers collided over instructional issues under the mounting pressure of demands to raise test scores.

In December, I invited parents to participate in a series of four interviews about reading. To identify parents, I started at the top of my class list and called parents until I had located nine parents were willing to be interviewed and who were willing to allow me to interview their children. Because there were a few families in my class who did not have a telephone, I contacted the remaining parent in person. Every parent I contacted agreed to participate in the study.

Interviews with parents were held at either the parents' homes or on a few occasions at their places of employment. In most cases children were interviewed at school with a few exceptions when it was more convenient to speak with the child at home. All interviews were transcribed in full.

In addition to the field notes and the interviews, I audiotaped our class discussions approximately once a week and saved copies of each student's first grade portfolio, which included running records, dictated sentences, writing samples, and self-portraits. In January, I realized that interesting and productive conversations were being held during our guided reading groups. I began audiotaping these as well. My goal was to create a grounded theory model of the reading process that incorporated the concepts about reading possessed by urban families. A grounded theory methodology requires that the findings of a study evolve directly from the data collected. Thus, I started with the data, coded the data based on categories inherent in the data, and used these categories to inform my construction of a model of the reading process.

As I struggled through the long process of transcribing the interviews and the classroom data, I kept note of ideas and issues raised by parents and students. I noted themes that reoccurred across interviews and noted points in the interviews when I found myself surprised by what I heard.

Once the data were transcribed, I coded the data using the codes I had identified during the transcription process as well as additional codes that emerged as I carefully reread the data. I used a data analysis computer program to place sections of data into separate files for each code. By the time I had coded all the data from the interviews, the classroom data, and my field notes, I had over fifty files. These code files were grouped into larger categories, which made the process more manageable and significantly less overwhelming.

Once the data were grouped into these larger categories, three major themes were immediately apparent: data exploring the roles reading plays in my students' families, data focusing on people's identities as readers, and data examining the relationships people share around reading. Each of these themes became a chapter in my earlier book, *Reading Families: The Literate Lives of Urban Children* (Compton-Lilly 2003). As I wrote that book, it became apparent that connections and relationships between these categories, the home and school contexts, and the various ways people spoke about reading revealed larger themes that became the basis of the model of reading presented in that book. This model allows for a deeper understanding of the complexities that surround the process of learning to read in an urban community.

While my first book allowed me to present my findings to the academic community, I worried that my fellow teachers would not hear my message. Thus, the book you are reading was written. In this book, I use the data to illustrate various themes that arose during the research study and to dispel various myths about urban families and reading. I have offered classroom examples that will hopefully help teachers build on the funds of knowledge that their students bring. In this current book, have slightly edited the words of parents and children for the sake of clarity by removing repetitions and false starts and editing out tangential comments.

REFERENCES

Allington, Richard, ed. 2002. *Big Brother and the National Reading Curriculum: How Ideology Trumped Evidence.* Portsmouth, NH: Heinemann.

Barton, D. and M. Hamilton. 1998. *Local Literacies: Reading and Writing in One Community.* London: Routledge.

Blackwell, Jeffrey. 2003. "Robbery Motive in Killing, Cops Say." *Democrat and Chronicle,* January 1, 1B.

Brooks, S. 2000. "Poverty and Environmentally Induced Damage to Children." In *The Public Assault on America's Children: Poverty, Violence, and Juvenile Injustice,* edited by V. Polakow. New York: Teachers College Press.

Coles, Gerald. 2003. *Reading the Naked Truth: Literacy, Legislation, and Lies.* Portsmouth, NH: Heinemann.

Compton-Lilly, Catherine. 2003. *Reading Families: The Literate Lives of Urban Children.* New York: Teachers College Press.

Delpit, Lisa. 1995. *Other People's Children.* New York: The New Press.

Fairclough, Norman. 1989. *Language and Power.* New York: Longman.

Freebody, Peter, Tim Forrest, and Stephanie Gunn. 2001. "Accounting and Silencing in Interviews:Smooth Running Through the 'Problem of Schooling the Disadvantaged.'" In *Difference, Silence, and Textual Practice,* edited by P. Freebody, S. Muspratt, and B. Dwyer. Cresskill, NJ: Hampton Press.

Freire, Paulo. 1986. *Pedagogy of the Oppressed.* New York: Continuum.

Gans, Herbert. 1995. *The War Against the Poor.* New York: Basic Books.

Garan, Elaine. 2002. *Resisting Reading Mandates: How to Triumph with the Truth.* Portsmouth, NH: Heinemann.

Garbarino, James, Nancy Dubrow, Kathleen Kostelny, and Carole Pardo. 1992. *Children in Danger: Coping with the Consequences of Community Violence.* San Francisco: Jossey-Bass.

Gee, James Paul. 1990. *Social Linguistics and Literacies: Ideologies in Discourses*. London: Falmer Press.

————. 1992. *The Social Mind: Language, Ideology and Social Practice*. New York: Bergin and Garvey.

————. 1998. *An Introduction to Discourse Analysis: Theory and Method*. London: Routledge.

Giroux, Henry A. 1992. "Critical Literacy and Student Experience: Donald Graves' Approach to Literacy." In *Becoming Political*, edited by P. Shannon. Portsmouth, NH: Heinemann.

Gould, Stephen Jay. 1981. *The Mismeasure of Man*. New York: W.W. Norton and Company.

Gregory, Eve. and Ann Williams. 2000. *City Literacies: Learning to Read Across Generations and Cultures*. London, Routledge.

Gutierrez, K., P. Baquedano-Lopez, and C. Tejeda. 1999. "Rethinking Diversity: Hybridity and Hybrid Language Practices in the Third Space." *Mind Culture and Activity* 6 (4):286–303.

Gutierrez, Kris, Patricia Baquedano-Lopez, and Myrna Gwen Turner. 2001. "Putting Language Back in Language Arts: When the Radical Middle Meets the Third Space." In *Becoming Political, Too*, edited by P. Shannon. Portsmouth, NH: Heinemann.

Hymes, Dell. 1996. *Ethnography, Linguistics, Narrative, Inequality: Toward an Understanding of Voice*. London: Taylor and Francis.

Johnson, Tammy, Jennifer Emiko Boyden, and William J. Pittz. 2001. "Racial Profiling in U. S. Schools." October 30, 2001 [cited November 5, 2001].

Lankshear, Colin, and Peter McLaren. 1993. *Critical Literacy: Politics, Praxis, and the Postmodern*. Albany, NY: State University of New York Press.

Lyon, Reid. 1997. "Presentation at the Hearing on Literacy. Committee of Education and the Workforce of the House of Representatives.

Milne, A. A. 1992. *Now We Are Six*. New York: Dutton's Children's Books.

Moll, L. C., C. Amanti, D. Neff, and N. Gonzalez. 1992. "Funds of Knowledge for Teaching: Using a Qualitative Approach to Connect Homes and Classrooms." *Theory into Practice* 31 (2):132–141.

Moss, Beverly J. 2001. "From the Pews to the Classrooms: Influences of the African American Church of Academic Literacy." In *Literacy in African American Communities*, edited by J. L. Harris, A. G. Kamhi, and K. E. Pollock. Mahwah, NJ: Lawrence Erlbaum.

National Institute of Environmental Health Services. 1997. www.niehs.nih-gov/od/K-12home.htm [cited 2001].

National Reading Panel. 2000a. *National Reading Panel: Teaching Children to Read: An Evidence-Based Assessment of the Scientific Research Literature on Reading and Its Implications for Reading Instruction: Reports of the Subgroups*. Washington, DC: U.S. Department of Health and Human Services, Public Health Service, National Institutes of Health, National Institute of Child Health and Human Development.

————. 2000b. *Teaching Children to Read: An Evidence-Based Assessment of the Scientific Research Literature on Reading and Its Implications for Instruction* [Summary of the Reports of the Subgroups]. Washington, DC: U. S. Department of Health and Human Services, Public Health Service, National Institutes of Health, National Institute of Child Health and Human Development.

New Standards. 2000. "What Parents Need to Know About Reading and Writing Grade by Grade: Literacy in Kindergarten Through Third Grade." Pittsburgh, PA: National Center for Education and the Economy and the University of Pittsburgh.

Nieto, Sonia. 1996. *Affirming Diversity: The Sociopolitical Context of Multicultural Education*, 2nd ed. White Plains, NY: Longman.

————. 1999. *The Light in Their Eyes*. New York: Teachers College Press.

Shannon, Patrick. 2001. *iShop You Shop: Raising Questions About Reading Commodities*. Portsmouth, NH: Heinemann.

————. 2002. "We Can Work It Out." In *Education, Inc. Turning Learning into a Business*, edited by A. Kohn and P. Shannon. Portsmouth, NH: Heinemann.

Skilton-Sylvester, Paul. 1999. "Teaching Without Charisma:Involving Third Graders as Co-investigators of Their Inner-City Neighborhood." In *Making Justice Our Project:Teachers Working Toward Critical Whole Language Practice*, edited by C. Edelsky. Urbana, IL: National Council of Teachers of English.

Taylor, Denny. 2000. "Making Literacy Webs in Schools, Families, and Communities." *School Talk: Between the Ideal and Real World of Teaching*. 6 (1):1–2.

Washington, Julie A., and Holly K. Craig. 2001. "Reading Performance and Dialectical Variation." In *Literacy in African American Communities*, edited by J. Harris, A. G. Kamhi, and K. E. Pollock. Mahwah, NJ: Lawrence Erlbaum.

INDEX